Camping
Morocco

We are very grateful that users of our guides write letters and emails to us, praising or criticising entries or recommending new entries. Please make the effort to send your comments and help us make the next edition even better.

Special thanks to Chris & Freda Gladman.

First published in Great Britain by Vicarious Books Ltd, 2009.

This edition published September 2009.

Vicarious Books Ltd, 62 Tontine Street, Folkestone, Kent, CT20 1JP. Tel:0131 2083333.
www.VicariousBooks.co.uk

Editors: Meli George and Chris Doree.

Inspectors: Andy & Nette Clarke from ukmotorhomes.net

Design and artwork by: Chris Gladman Design 07745 856652.

Printed in the UK.

Morocco is just one hour by ferry from Spain, but disembarking travellers find they have entered life from a bygone age, everything seems different yet familiar. There are people dressed in suits but many more wearing pointy hooded cloaks. On the chaotic roads modern cars jostle for position with donkey carts. This is just the beginning of an amazing journey of discovery into lands and cultures that have not been ravaged by modernisation. With this guide no matter what you do or where you go during the day you can be confident that your evening destination is going to be exactly where it says it is and the site is going to be good, bad or indifferent as described.

Morocco's climate makes it great for camping, especially if you take your own vehicle and go and explore this fascinating country. The open roads and dramatic scenery will appeal to all adventurers whether they travel by bicycle, motorcycle, car, 4x4, camper or motorhome. This is a campsite guide for everyone, all the sites are open all year and accessible by any form of transport.

Morocco is an all year round destination, but camping during the summer may be too hot for some, so if you don't want to boil in the bag the best months to visit are from October until June. Increasing numbers of campers are visiting during the winter months; most people drive the Atlantic coast, some in search of warm winter sunshine and others looking for Atlantic surf. All the open all year campsites and surf spots along the coast were visited in 2009 and have been listed in the guide.

Andy and Nette Clarke undertook extensive Moroccan campsite inspections from January to April 2009. They gathered a wealth of essential information before and during their 14000km journey, the important and useful bits gleaned are provided here for future over-land travellers.

MAP OF MOROCCO

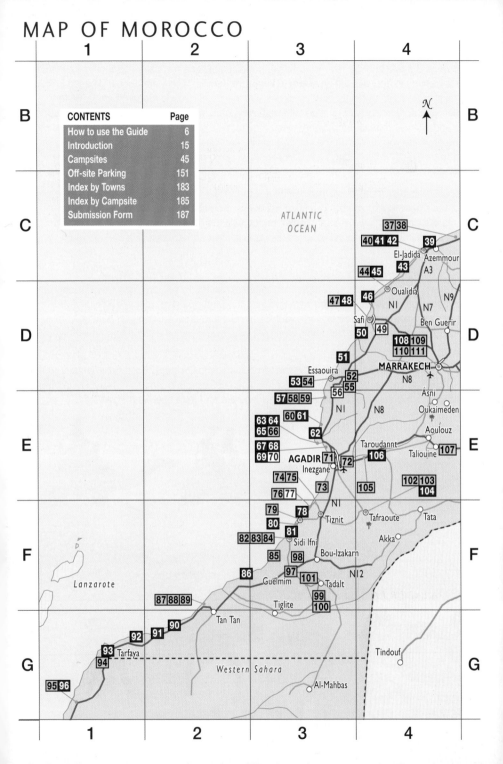

CONTENTS	Page
How to use the Guide	6
Introduction	15
Campsites	45
Off-site Parking	151
Index by Towns	183
Index by Campsite	185
Submission Form	187

MAP OF MOROCCO

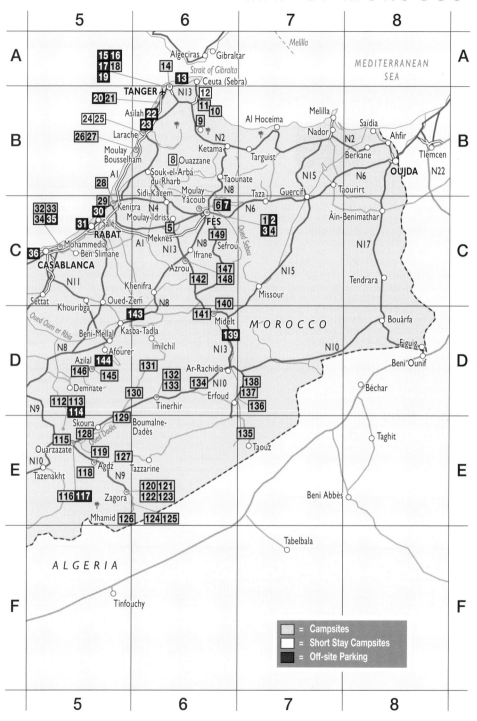

HOW TO USE THIS GUIDE

Français
1. Introduction L'introduction fournit tout ce que vous devez savoir, des visas d'entrée aux achats de nourriture.

2. Cartes Page 4, une carte générale présente tous les sites de ce guide; (par exemple 11-12-13 près de Tanger). Au début de chaque chapitre, une carte présente les sites appropriés.

3. Informations détaillées Les sites sont identifiés et classés par le nom de ville. Utilisant le même numéro que les cartes pour chaque chapitre, les sites sont classés en ordre croissant.

4. A l'arrière du guide, vous trouverez un index reprenant le nom de ville et le nom de terrain de camping. N'oubliez pas de nous renvoyer le questionnaire également à l'arrière.

Description - chaque site est décrit de façon impartiale. Les points positifs et points faibles de l'emplacement sont fournis, ainsi que toutes les informations utiles.

Logement de vacances - quelques terrains de camping ont des logements à la location : tentes, appartements. Ces locations n'ont pas été inspectées.

Coordonnées GPS - au format N35°31.926 W005°59.920. Il est peu probable que votre GPS ait la cartographie du Maroc.

Deutsch
1. Einleitung Die Einleitung liefert alles, das Sie von den Einreisevisa zum Kauf der Nahrung wissen müssen.

2. Diagramme Auf Seite 4, identifizieren ein Überblickdiagramm die Positionen aller Auflistungen in diesem Führer; sehen Sie 11-12-13 nahe Tanger. Zu Beginn jedes Kapitels identifizieren ein Diagramm nur die relevanten Auflistungen.

3. Ausführliche Information Aufstellungsorte werden durch Stadtnamen identifiziert und verzeichnet. Unter Verwendung der gleichen Zahlen wie auf den Diagrammen in jedem Kapitel sind die Aufstellungsorte registriertes mit der niedrigsten Zahl numerisch beginnen und beenden auf dem höchsten.

4. Ein Index, der durch Stadtnamen und Campingplatznamen verzeichnet wird, kann an der Rückseite gefunden werden. Vergessen Sie nicht, die Unterordnungform an der Rückseite auch einzureichen.

Beschreibung - eine unparteiische Beschreibung wird über den Aufstellungsort gegeben. Die Stärken oder die Schwächen und der Anklang des Aufstellungsortes werden zur Verfügung gestellt. Weitere nützliche Informationen werden auch gegeben.

Feiertags-Anpassung - einige Campingplätze haben Anpassung für Miete, schwankt dieser von Zelte zu Wohnungen, aber ist nicht geprüft.

GPS koordiniert - diese werden im N35°31.926 W005°59.920 Format dargestellt. Es ist Ihre GPS-Maschine hat das Marokkodiagramm unwahrscheinlich.

Italiano
1. Introduzione L'introduzione fornisce tutto che dobbiate sapere dai visti di entrata a comprare l'alimento.

2. Programmi Alla pagina 4, un programma di descrizione identifica le posizioni di tutti gli elenchi in questa guida; vedi 11-12-13 vicino a Tangeri. All'inizio di ogni capitolo, un programma identifica soltanto gli elenchi relativi.

3. Informazioni dettagliate I luoghi sono identificati ed elencati dal nome della città. Utilizzando gli stessi numeri di sui programmi in ogni capitolo i luoghi sono numericamente cominciare elencato con il numero più basso, rifinente sull'più alto.

4. Un indice elencato dal nome della città e dal nome del campsite può essere trovato alla parte posteriore. Non dimentichi di presentare la forma di presentazione anche alla parte posteriore.

Descrizione - una descrizione imparziale è data circa il luogo. Le resistenze o le debolezze e l'appello del luogo sono forniti. Ulteriori informazioni utili inoltre sono fornite.

Sistemazione di festa - alcuni campsites hanno sistemazione per noleggio, questo varia dalle tende agli appartamenti, ma è non ispezionato.

Il GPS coordina - questi sono presentati nella disposizione di N35°31.926 W005°59.920. È improbabile la vostra macchina di GPS avrà tracciato del Marocco.

Español
1. Introducción La introducción proporciona todo que usted necesita saber de visas de entrada a comprar el alimento.

2. Mapas En la página 4, un mapa de la descripción identifica las localizaciones de todos los listados en esta guía; vea 11-12-13 cerca de Tánger. Al principio de cada capítulo, un mapa identifica solamente los listados relevantes.

3. Información detallada Los sitios son identificados y enumerados por nombre de la ciudad. Usando los mismos números que en los mapas en cada capítulo los sitios son numéricamente el comenzar enumerado con el número más bajo, acabando en el más alto.

4. Un índice enumeró por nombre de la ciudad y el nombre del sitio para acampar se puede encontrar en la parte posterior. No olvide presentar el impreso de la sumisión también en la parte posterior.

Descripción - una descripción imparcial se da sobre el sitio. Las fuerzas o las debilidades y la súplica del sitio se proporcionan. La información útil adicional también se da.

Comodidad del día de fiesta - algunos sitios para acampar tienen comodidad para el alquiler, éste varía de las tiendas a los apartamentos, pero es sin inspeccionar.

El GPS coordina - éstos se presentan en el formato de N35°31.926 W005°59.920. Es inverosímil su máquina del GPS tendrá trazado de Marruecos.

HOW TO USE THIS GUIDE

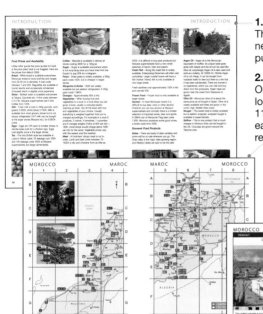

1. Introduction
The introduction provides everything you need to know from entry visas to purchasing food.

2. Maps
On page 4, an overview map identifies the locations of all the listings in this guide; see 11-12-13 near Tanger. At the beginning of each chapter, a map identifies only the relevant listings.

Holiday Accommodation – Some campsites have accommodation for hire, this varies from tents to apartments, but is un-inspected.

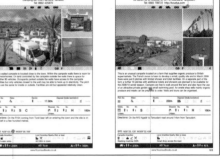

3. Detailed Information
Sites are identified and listed by town name. Using the same numbers as on the maps in each chapter the sites are listed numerically starting with the lowest number, finishing on the highest.

Description – An unbiased description is given about the site. The strengths or weaknesses and appeal of the site are provided. Further useful information is also given.

GPS Co-ordinates – These are presented in the N35°31.926' W005°59.920' format. It is unlikely your GPS machine will have Morocco mapping.

4. Index and Submission Forms
An index listed by town name and campsite name can be found at the rear. Don't forget to submit the submission form also at the rear.

HOW TO USE THIS GUIDE

Explanation of a campsite entry (also see key to symbols on pages 10 and 11)

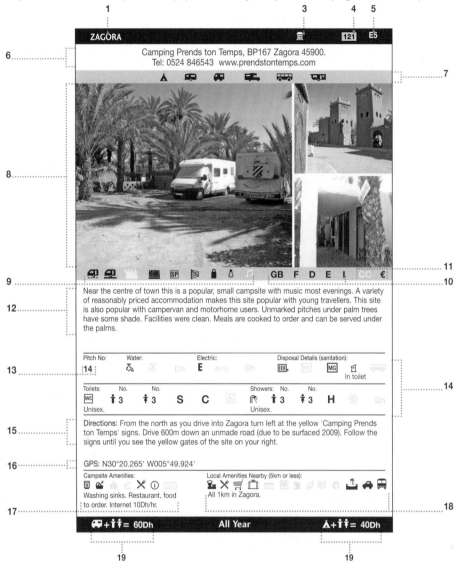

Near the centre of town this is a popular, small campsite with music most evenings. A variety of reasonably priced accommodation makes this site popular with young travellers. This site is also popular with campervan and motorhome users. Unmarked pitches under palm trees have some shade. Facilities were clean. Meals are cooked to order and can be served under the palms.

Pitch No:	Water:		Electric:		Disposal Details (sanitation):		
14	♨	Dh	E Amp	Dh	IIII, MG	MG	In toilet

Toilets:	No.	No.		Showers:	No.	No.	
WC Unisex.	♀3	♂3	S C	♀3	♂3	H	Dh Unisex.

Directions: From the north as you drive into Zagora turn left at the yellow 'Camping Prends ton Temps' signs. Drive 600m down an unmade road (due to be surfaced 2009). Follow the signs until you see the yellow gates of the site on your right.

GPS: N30°20.265' W005°49.924'

Campsite Amenities:	Local Amenities Nearby (5km or less):
Washing sinks. Restaurant, food to order. Internet 10Dh/hr.	All 1km in Zagora.

+♀♂= 60Dh — **All Year** — **+♀♂= 40Dh**

Español

1 Nombre de la ciudad
2 Tipo del estacionamiento
3 Ambiente
4 Número del mapa
5 Referencia de rejilla
6 Nombre del sitio para acampar, dirección, número de teléfono y Web site
7 Las unidades aceptaron
8 Fotografías del sitio
9 Características
10 Idiomas
11 Euros de las tarjetas de crédito aceptados
12 Descripción
13 Número de echadas
14 Instalaciones
15 Direcciones
16 El GPS coordina
17 Amenidades del sitio para acampar
18 Amenidades locales
19 Precio 2009
20 Detalles y cargas para el servicio

Explanation of an off-site parking entry (also see key to symbols on pages 10 and 11)

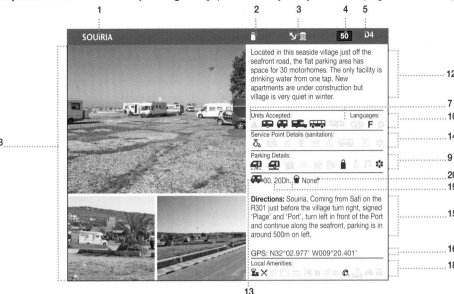

English
1 Town Name
2 Parking type
3 Ambience
4 Map Number
5 Grid reference
6 Campsite name, address, telephone number and website
7 Units accepted
8 Site photographs
9 Features
10 Languages
11 Credit cards/ Euros accepted
12 Description
13 Number of pitches
14 Facilities
15 Directions
16 GPS Co-ordinates
17 Campsite amenities
18 Local amenities
19 Price in 2009
20 Details and charges for service

Français
1 Nom de ville
2 Type de stationnement
3 Ambiance
4 Nombre de carte
5 Référence de grille
6 Nom de terrain de camping, adresse, numéro de téléphone et site Web
7 Unités admises
8 Photographies d'emplacement
9 Dispositifs
10 Langues
11 Les euros de cartes de crédit ont accepté
12 Description
13 Nombre de lancements
14 Équipements
15 Directions
16 Le GPS coordonne
17 Agréments de terrain de camping
18 Agréments locaux
19 Prix 2009
20 Détails et frais pour le service

Deutsch
1 Stadtname
2 Parkenart
3 Ambiente
4 Diagramm-Zahl
5 Gitterkoordinaten
6 Campingplatzname, Adresse, Telefonnummer und Web site
7 Maßeinheiten angenommen
8 Aufstellungsortfotographien
9 Eigenschaften
10 Sprachen
11 Kreditkarten Euro nahmen an
12 Beschreibung
13 Zahl der Taktabstände
14 Anlagen
15 Richtungen
16 GPS koordiniert
17 Campingplatzannehmlichkeiten
18 Lokale Annehmlichkeiten
19 Preis 2009
20 Details und Gebühren für Service

Italiano
1 Nome della città
2 Tipo di parcheggio
3 Atmosfera
4 Numero del programma
5 Riferimento di griglia
6 Nome del Campsite, indirizzo, numero di telefono e Web site
7 Le unità hanno accettato
8 Fotografie del luogo
9 Caratteristiche
10 Lingue
11 Gli euro delle carte di credito hanno accettato
12 Descrizione
13 Numero dei passi
14 Facilità
15 Sensi
16 Il GPS coordina
17 Amenità del Campsite
18 Amenità locali
19 Prezzo 2009
20 Particolari e spese per servizio

HOW TO USE THIS GUIDE

KEY TO SYMBOLS	CLEF AUX SYMBOLS	SCHLÜSSEL ZU DEN SYMBOLEN	CHIAVE AI SIMBOLI	LLAVE A LOS SÍMBOLOS
English	**Français**	**Deutsch**	**Italiano**	**Español**
Tent	Tente	Zelt	Tenda	Tienda
Touring Caravan	Tourisme de la caravane	Reisen des Wohnwagens	Visita del caravan	Viajar la caravana
Motorhome 6m	Camping Car 6m	Reisemobil 6m	Camper 6m	Autocaravana 6m
Motorhome 6-8m	Camping Car 6-8m	Reisemobil 6-8m	Camper 6-8m	Autocaravana 6-8m
Motorhome 8+	Camping Car 8+	Reisemobil 8+	Camper 8+	Autocaravana 8+
Accomodation for hire	Logement pour la location	Anpassung für Miete	Sistemazione per noleggio	Comodidad para el alquiler
Guarded	Gardé	Geschützt	Custodetto	Guardado
Surf	Vague déferlante	Brandung	Spuma	Resaca
Day Parking	Stationnement de jour	Tagesparken	Parcheggio di giorno	Estacionamiento del día
Coastal	Côtier	Küsten	Litoraneo	Costa
Residential	Résidentiel	Wohn	Residenziale	Residencial
Urban	Urbain	Städtisch	Urbano	Urbano
Rural	Rural	Landwirtschaftlich	Rurale	Rural
Village	Village	Dorf	Villaggio	Aldea
Riverside/lakeside	Riviere/lac	Fluss/See	Fiume/lago	Río/ lago
Farm	Fermea	Bauernhof	Azienda agricola	Granja
Hard standing Pitches	Lancements durs de position	Harte Stellung Taktabstände	Passi duri di condizione	Echadas duras de l a situación
Level Pitches	Lancements de niveau	Niveau-Taktabstände	Passi del livello	Echadas del nivel
Grass	Herbe	Gras	Erba	Hierba
Sand	Sable	Sand	Sabbia	Arena
Shaded parking	Stationnement ombragé	Schattiertes Parken	Parcheggio protetto	Estacionamiento sombreado
Illuminated	Illuminé	Belichtet	Illuminato	Iluminado
Fenced	Clôturé	Gefochten	Recintato	Cercado
Noisy	Bruyant	Laut	Rumoroso	Ruidoso
Open all year	Ouvrez toute l'année	Öffnen Sie alles Jahr	Apra tutto l'anno	Abra todo el año
Water	L'eau	Wasser	Acqua	Agua
Non drinking water	Eau non potable	Nicht Trinkwasser	Acqua potabile non	Agua no potable
Electric hook up	Connexion électrique	Elektrischer Haken oben	Collegamento elettrico	Gancho eléctrico para arriba
Grey water disposal	Disposition grise de l'eau	Graue Wasserbeseitigung	Eliminazione grigia dell'acqua	Disposición gris del agua
Toilet disposal	Disposition de toilette	Toilettenbeseitigung	Eliminazione della toletta	Disposición del tocador
Motorhome grey water disposal	Disposition grise de l'eau de camping car	Wohnmobil graue Wasserbeseitigung	Eliminazione grigia dell'acqua di camper	Disposición gris del agua de Autocaravana
Motorhome toilet waste disposal	Évacuation des déchets de toilette de camping car	Müllentsorgung der wohnmobil Toilette	Eliminazione dei rifiuti della toletta di camper	Disposición inútil del tocador de Autocaravana
Toilets	Toilettes	Toiletten	Tolette	Tocadores
Disabled toilet	Toilette handicapée	Untaugliche Toilette	Toleta disabile	Tocador lisiado

	English	Français	Deutsch	Italiano	Español
Ṫ	Male	Mâle	Mann	Maschio	Varón
Ṫ	Female	Femelle	Frau	Femmina	Hembra
S	Standard toilet	Toilette standard	Standardtoilette	Toletta standard	Tocador estándar
C	Continental toilet	Toilette continentale	Kontinentale Toilette	Toletta continentale	Tocador continental
	Showers	Douches	Duschen	Acquazzoni	Duchas
H	Hot	Chaud	Heiß	Caldo	Caliente
❄	Cold	Froid	Kalt	Freddo	Frío
GB	English	Anglais	Englisch	Inglese	Inglés
I	Italian	Italien	Italienisch	Italiano	Italiano
F	French	Français	Französisch	Francese	Francés
S	Swedish	Suédois	Schwedisch	Svedese	Sueco
D	German	Allemand	Deutsch	Tedesco	Alemán
E	Spanish	Espagnol	Spanisch	Spagnolo	Español
CC	Credit cards	Cartes de credit	Kreditkarten	Carte di credito	Tarjetas de crédito
€€	Euros	Euros	Euro	Euro	Euros
	Laundry	Blanchisserie	Wäscherei	Lavanderia	Lavadero
✗	Restaurant	Restaurant	Gaststätte	Ristorante	Restaurante
	Dishwashing facilities	Équipements de vaisselle	Abwaschanlagen	Facilità di lavatura dei piatti	Instalaciones del lavaplatos
(i)	Internet	Internet	Internet	Internet	Internet
	Shop	Magasin	Geschäft	Negozio	Tienda
WiFi	WiFI	WiFi	WiFi	WiFi	WiFi
	Swimming pool	Piscine	Schwimmbad	Piscina)	Piscina
	Provisions	Dispositions	Bestimmungen	Disposizioni	Provisiones
	Camping Shop	Magasin campant	Kampierendes Geschäft	Negozio di campeggio	Tienda que acampa
	Gas	Gaz	Gas	Gas	Gas
	4x4 trips	Voyages 4x4	Reisen 4x4	Viaggi 4x4	Viajes 4x4
M	Market (souk)	Marché (souk)	Markt (souk)	Mercato (souk)	Mercado (souk)
	Public transport	Transport en commun	Öffentliche Transportmittel	Trasporto pubblico	Transporte público
	Supermarket	Supermarché	Supermarkt	Supermercato	Supermercado
	Tourist attraction	Attraction touristique	Touristenattraktion	Attrazione turistica	Atracción turística
	Beach	Plage	Strand	Spiaggia	Playa
	Bank ATM	Banque	Bank ATM	Atmosfera della Banca	Atmósfera del banco
	Camel Trips	Voyages de chameau	Kamel-Reisen	Viaggi del cammello	Viajes del camello

Note: Facilities only available when symbol highlighted.

Note : Équipements seulement disponibles quand le symbole a accentué.

Anmerkung: Anlagen nur vorhanden, als Symbol hervorhob.

Nota: Facilità soltanto disponibili quando il simbolo ha evidenziato.

Nota: Instalaciones solamente disponibles cuando el simbolo destacó.

Drinking water: Although some piped water may be indicated as 'eau potable' (drinking water), it is advised that it should all be regarded as not suitable for drinking unless you have an adequate water purifier/filter fitted. Bottled water is readily available. Using disinfectant wipes or spray before drawing water will improve hygiene. Tap fittings vary widely in type and size.

Grey Water: In Morocco drive-over grey water disposal points are rare. A receptacle will be required to transport grey water to an appropriate disposal point. If a drive-over grid is available care should be taken not to cause any damage, especially with heavy motorhomes. Take a length of flexible pipe to direct water accurately.

Toilet disposal: Only use the designated facility, lifting or flipping up grids before emptying. This is sometimes marked with 'Cassette'. Do not rush toilet emptying, as spillage will occur. Ensure that any mess is cleaned up and NEVER use the fresh water tap to rinse toilet cassettes.

Fixed tank toilet systems are rarely catered for. It is your responsibility to organise your disposal to suit these widely varying systems. A flexible pipe will often be required to reach the drain but should be used to ensure accurate waste disposal and a macerator is recommended.

Parking

Parking is on a first come first served basis. It is not possible to reserve a space. Always park in designated bays if provided and never obstruct roadways or service points. If the parking is full find another one. When provided always park in allotted spaces, not in another place that you prefer the look of. Never put out camping equipment or awnings on municipal parking areas. Remember it is parking not camping.

Motorway Service Stations are similar in style to European ones, though smaller. We do not advise staying overnight on them.

Change is inevitable and Morocco is developing quickly yet the old ways still dominate life. Expect things to change at short notice or without notice at all. Campsite facilities may have become run down or possibly improved. Sites may have closed and new ones have popped up within a few months. Please let us know by filling in one of the report forms in the back of the guide, we also need to know if things stay the same.

Vicarious Books Ltd cannot be held accountable for the quality, safety or operation of the site concerned, or for the fact that conditions, facilities, management or prices may have changed.

Vicarious Books

All The Aires
SPAIN AND PORTUGAL

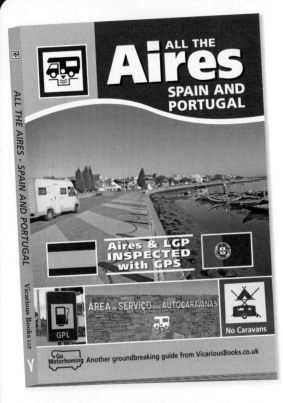

- More Aires than any other guide
- Inspected and photographed
- Easy directions, on-site GPS co-ordinates
- Directions with road names, numbers and postcodes
- Aires for big motorhomes

only **£11.99**
inc UK P&P

In Spain and Portugal, motorhomes have the privilege of staying on 'Àrea de Serviço para Autocaravanas'. These are special areas providing facilities for motorhomes in the form of overnight parking and/or service point for water collection and disposal of waste fluids. These can be free or cost a few Euros. Aires symbolise the freedom of motorhoming. You are welcomed into local communities, where you can stay overnight at unique locations unavailable to other travellers.

To order, give us a call or visit our website to buy online.

0131 208 3333 **www.VicariousBooks.co.uk**

INTRODUCTION

Before you go

Being spontaneous is part of the essence of travelling. When looking across the Straits of Gibraltar, Morocco is temptingly close. But hold your horses, Morocco is not part of the EU and standard European travel arrangements may not be sufficient, for example, pets including horses are not covered by the pet passport scheme. A little preparation before your visit will enhance your trip.

Passports and Visas

Passports must remain valid for at least six months after your entry date into Morocco. EU citizens do not require a visa for entry into Morocco but your passport will be stamped with a unique number. This number is your official identity and may be a required field on any form you fill in including campsite booking in forms. Identity numbers may also be checked at police or military check points. You are free to travel for three months from date of entry. Non-EU citizens should confirm visa requirements in advance.

Travel Insurance

The EHIC card is not valid in Morocco. Travel insurance that covers medical and other emergencies should be considered essential. The travel insurance market is competitive, so an inexpensive policy with an acceptable level of cover can easily be purchased. Check the territorial limits as some policies include Morocco in their definition of Europe, and a 'Europe' policy is likely to be cheaper than one covering 'Africa' or a 'Worldwide' policy.

Inoculations

No injections are required prior to visiting Morocco, but it is worth considering having the following: Tetanus, Hepatitis A, Typhoid Fever, Diphtheria, Polio, Rabies and Tuberculosis. The editors have inspected thousands of toilet emptying points and recommend that you be inoculated against diseases that are carried in human waste.

Pets

Morocco is not part of the EU, and is not a qualifying 'non-European Union country' under the Pet Passport Scheme, therefore dogs, cats and ferrets etc. cannot return to the EU under the scheme. It is possible to take a pet to Morocco from Spain and return with it without the necessity for quarantine, but an International Veterinary Certificate is required. Our advice is that you do not consider taking your pet to Morocco, if you do want to take a pet you must ensure that you fully understand, and comply with, the relevant Spanish, Moroccan, and UK regulations.

INTRODUCTION

<table>
<tr><td colspan="2">

ATTESTATION D'ASSURANCE OBLIGATOIRE DES VEHICULES TERRESTRES A MOTEUR

(Article 2 de l'arrêté du ministre des finances et de la privatisation n° 213-05 du 26 janvier 2005)

</td><td colspan="2">

شهادة التأمين الإجباري على العربات البرية ذات محرك

(المادة 2 من قرار وزير المالية و الخوصصة رقم 213.05 الصادر في 26 يناير 2005)

</td></tr>
</table>

ASSURANCE AUX FRONTIERES	التأمين بالحدود
NUMERO D'ORDRE	الرقم الترتيبي
Usage	الاستعمال

PROPRIETAIRE DU VEHICULE — مالك العربة

Nom	الاسم
N° du passeport ou de la carte d'identité nationale	رقم جواز السفر او بطاقة التعريف الوطنية
Adresse	العنوان

POLICE D'ASSURANCE — بوليصة التأمين

Entreprise d'assurances	**شركة تأمين النقل** COMPAGNIE D'ASSURANCE TRANSPORT 6، لاكولين سيدي معروف – الدار البيضاء	مقاولة التأمين
Numéro de la police		رقم البوليصة
Intermédiaire		الوسيط

VEHICULE — العربة

N° d'immatriculation		رقم التسجيل
A défaut, N° du moteur ou		عند عدم وجوده ، رقم المحرك
N° du chassis		او رقم الهيكل
Marque et type		النوع و الشكل
Type de carrosserie		نوع الهيكل
Poids total en charge		الوزن الإجمالي مع الحمولة
Remorques		المقطورات
Nombre de places (véhicule + remorques)		عدد المقاعد (العربة+المقطورات)

PERIODE DE GARANTIE		Jour / اليوم	Mois / الشهر	Année / السنة		مدة الضمان
	DU:				من:	
	AU:				الى:	

Le présent document fait présumer que l'obligation d'assurance prévue à l'article 120 de la loi n° 17-99 portant code des assurances a été satisfaite pour la période de garantie indiquée ci-dessus.

يفترض من هذه الوثيقة ان إجبارية التأمين المنصوص عليها في المادة 120 من القانون رقم 17-99 المتعلق بمدونة التأمينات قد استوفيت لمدة الضمان المبينة اعلاه.

A TETOUAN   le   Pour l'assureur :

المملكة المغربية   في   عن المؤمن:

20 درهما

91 F / 58.900 / 06.08 / I03

Taking Vehicles to Morocco

All drivers must have a valid licence with them, a UK or EU Driving licence is sufficient, and there is no need for an International Driving Permit. The rear of your vehicle must display the nationality letters indicating its country of registration i.e. GB for Great Britain. The nationality indication on a standard EU style licence plate is not sufficient, so an adhesive decal should be on display.

V5C Vehicle Registration Document - The vehicle must be registered in the name, and at the address, of one of the vehicle occupants. European hire companies are unlikely to allow their hired motorhomes to be taken to Morocco. Motorhomes can be hired in Morocco from Camping Car Maroc (see page 105), located near Marrakech.

Vehicle insurance - Green Card - Some UK insurance companies will not issue a Green Card for Morocco and some policies only provide third party cover and others do not include the Western Sahara. Check your policy now before you forget and be prepared to change your policy if necessary.

Assurance Frontieres – If the geographical limits of your vehicle insurance do not extend to Morocco it is possible to buy 'Assurance Frontieres' on entry into Morocco, see form on left hand page. Assurance Frontieres only provides the minimum legally required insurance, i.e. liability to third parties. When entering Morocco at Tangier, the office is on the right just after the Customs. When entering from Ceuta, Assurance Frontieres are not available at the border but can be purchased in Tetouan. The easiest way to achieve this is to drive (carefully!) to the campsite at Martil and from there take a 'grand taxi', from the end of the road that goes past the campsite, to Tetouan. The taxi is shared and will cost 5Dh per person. You will be dropped at the western end of Bvd. Sidi Idris (all taxis to and from M'diq and Martil stop here). You need to head into town

across the Cajigas Gardens and find the Cinema Espagnol on Ave. Mohamed Torres. Almost opposite the cinema is an arcade, where you will find Assurances Randa, the staff there can issue Assurances Frontieres.

Their contact details are:

Assurances Randa S.A.R.L.
Siége Social 2,
Ave. Mohamed Torres,
Tetouan.
Tel: 0539 965602

In Jan 2009 buying Assurances Frontieres for one month cost 1000Dh, and 3 months cost 1950Dh. Payment must be made in cash and you will need to show your V5C Registration Document, your Passport, and the Vehicle Temporary Import Form.

Breakdown Cover - Insurers that provide Green Card cover for Morocco may also be able to provide breakdown cover, failing that, the only companies that we know of that provide this service are International Breakdown (www.internationalbreakdown.com) and the ADAC (www.adac.de). Ensure that cover offered is sufficient for your needs, restrictions may be applied to vehicle age or size or weight. Roadside assistance is unlikely to be available. You may be required to arrange your own recovery and repairs then reclaim the costs at a later date. We have had very good reports of the recovery service provided by ADAC in Morocco. On entry into Morocco vehicle temporary import details are registered, then recorded in your passport, if you attempt to leave the country without your vehicle you are liable to pay Moroccan import duty. You must therefore ensure that either your breakdown cover, or your insurance, provides for the repatriation of the vehicle, or settlement of any customs duty liable, should you be unable to leave with the vehicle, for example if it has been written off.

Ferries to Morocco

To avoid a very long and difficult drive you will need to board a ferry with your vehicle to get to Morocco. Routes vary in duration and cost:

From Spain ferries cross from: Algeciras to Tangier and Ceuta www.trasmediterranea.es and www.frs.es

Tarifa to Tangier (Tanger) and Ceuta www.frs.es

Almeria to Melilla and Nador and Al Hoceima.

Malaga to Melilla.

Barcelona to Tangier www.gnv.it

From France ferries cross from Sete to Nador and Port Vendres to Tangier www.comarit.com

Ferries also travel from Genoa in Italy to Tangier www.gnv.it

Most people choose to take a ferry from Algeciras to either Ceuta or Tangier. Both routes have pros and cons. The 45 minute fast ferry to Ceuta is less expensive than the three hour ferry to Tangier. The main advantage of the crossing to Tangier is that temporary immigration paperwork and control is carried out on the ferry. The main disadvantage is that you disembark directly into the hustle and bustle of a large Moroccan city. Thankfully the main routes out of Tangier are reasonably well signed. Ceuta is an autonomous low tax region of Spain so you disembark from the ferry into familiar EU territory, the disadvantage is that there can be a bit more hassle at the border crossing into Morocco. Goods in Ceuta are slightly cheaper than in mainland Spain so you can take advantage of cheaper fuel and alcohol etc. In January 2009 the cost of diesel in Ceuta was €0.63 per litre this being about 30 percent cheaper than top grade diesel in Morocco.

Tickets - Ferry tickets purchased in advance are likely to cost more than tickets purchased on arrival in Algeciras. Prices change from day to day. Numerous establishments selling ferry tickets are seen on the routes approaching Algeciras, if you have the time it's worth checking these out. It is also possible to buy tickets directly at the port entrance.

One popular place to buy ferry tickets is 'Agence de Viages Normandie' (see photo opposite), this agency is located opposite the Carrefour supermarket at Palmones (exit 112 from the E-15 / A7). Juan Carlos Gutierrez, the proprietor of the ticket agency, speaks French and a little English. The agency can provide the necessary forms required for the border crossing. The ticket agency does not accept card payments but there is a bank with an ATM opposite. In January 2009, open return ferry ticket prices for a motorhome and 2 passengers was €230 via Ceuta and €275 via Tangier, in comparison Ceuta tickets bought at the port cost €290. There is room for a few motorhomes to park overnight in front of the ticket agency, and many motorhomes park in the Lidl car park, apparently without problem. Presumably Lidl are happy with this arrangement if people stock up with supplies such as food, beer and wine, but remember **you are only allowed to import 1 bottle of wine, 1 bottle of spirits and 200 cigarettes.** There is also a McDonald's nearby, for a last fast food fix.

Wherever you buy your tickets you should purchase an open return ferry ticket, so that you can make the return crossing whenever you want. Check the details carefully on the actual tickets issued, especially if they are a bargain price. We have heard that some people have been sold day return tickets, or those valid only for residents of Ceuta. Remember the old saying, "If it seems too good to be true, it probably is!"

Embarkation in Algeciras - In Algeciras, follow the 'Puerto' signs, then on entering the Port follow the signs for Ceuta or Tangier as appropriate. The actual route through the port seems to vary, just follow the signs and directions of the port officials. Beware of the 'port entry fee' scam. Rogues act as if they are employed by the port to collect entry fees. Drivers are asked for their papers and then a port entry fee is demanded. This is a con; once you have purchased your ferry tickets there is nothing more to pay.

Disembarkation in Ceuta - Having exited the port, if you want to fill up with fuel you will find several filling stations on the road to the left signed for Morocco. Near the port there is a supermarket.

INTRODUCTION

Crossing the border

Border procedures vary depending on whether you enter Morocco at Tangier or Ceuta.

For entry at Tangier the Police immigration formalities are normally completed on the ferry, at Ceuta you drive to the border a few kilometres out of Ceuta town.

At both borders, when entering and leaving the country, you are likely to be approached by unofficial 'helpers' who, after they have assisted with your paperwork, will demand payment. It is not necessary to pay anyone to help you get through the border, no matter how insistent they are. If you need help, ask one of the uniformed officials.

For either place of entry each person requires a Temporary Immigration form and the vehicle requires a Temporary Import form. These forms are available at the border but it is more convenient if you can pick up copies when you buy your tickets, thus the forms can be completed in advance.

The Vehicle Temporary Import form can be filled in (but not submitted) online, you may wish to do this before you leave home, visit

www.douane.gov.ma/EDouane/DMCV/AT/Formulaire_AT.asp

The following notes will help you complete the online form:

Prénom et Nom: First name and surname. Select 'Autres' if you have not been to Morocco before. If you have been before and have the Police registration number stamped in the last page of your passport, select 'Étrangers non résidant' and fill in the Police number in the box.

Immatriculation: Vehicle Registration number.

Marque: Make (as recorded on your V5C Registration Document).
Modèle: Model/Type (as on the V5C).
Genre: Select CAMPING-CAR (for a motorhome or campervan).

Pays: Select country of registration (e.g. GRANDE BRETAGNE).

Date de 1ère mise en circulation: Date of first registration (dd/mm/yyyy).

Châssis n°: Chassis number.

Select 'Imprimer' to prepare a page for printing, you will get three copies of the form, two on one sheet of paper and one on another. All three copies must be stamped at the Moroccan border; one is retained and two returned to you, these must be kept safe. When you leave the country with your vehicle, you will need to hand one copy in, the other is stamped on exit and is your proof that you have taken (exported) your vehicle out of the country.

It's a similar procedure if you pick up the form locally (it's a triplicate carbon copy NCR form). Fill it in at or before the border, the notes above will also help you complete the three-part form.

Formalities for entry at Tangier - Follow the directions of the port officials to the Customs building, if you have already filled in the vehicle temporary import forms just wait for a customs official to come to you to collect them. If you do not have Vehicle Temporary Import forms just ask any of the uniformed officials, or anyone with an official ID tag, for the forms you need, they will also help you fill them in if needed. Once completed and handed into customs you will get two stamped copies back, do not lose them! You will need them when you come to leave the country as explained above.

Formalities for entry from Ceuta - Do not leave your vehicle unattended whilst at the border, the area can be chaotic and thefts from vehicles are not uncommon. The procedure is similar to that at Tangier; you queue up with your vehicle until you reach the border post where you will need to visit two offices. One is the Police, here you will complete temporary immigration formalities, and the other is the Customs, where the temporary vehicle import formalities are completed. You can ask for help from one of the uniformed officials or anyone with an official ID tag.

INTRODUCTION

Driving and roads

Morocco is a country of contrasts and this is true of the road system. Main routes are generally good and motorways are up to European standards. New roads and improvements to popular tourist routes are currently underway. Many of the rural roads that benefit from tarmac are effectively single lane, comprising a tarmac strip one vehicle wide and rough compacted gravel 'hard shoulder' on either side. Often there is a sharp drop off the edge of the tarmac, consider this when meeting oncoming traffic. Morocco is popular with 4x4 and off-road bike enthusiasts because there are so many unmade tracks or pistes to go and explore. These tracks are mostly unmarked so good navigation skills are required.

The standard of driving in Morocco is poor, and dangerous driving may well be the most serious threat to your safety and health during your visit. Rural roads are generally quiet and easy to drive but town driving is a nerve-wracking experience and should be undertaken with great care. If you don't already practice defensive driving you would be well advised to start. Moroccan drivers often jump red lights, or come up to a line of stationary vehicles at traffic lights only to pull onto the wrong side of the road in an attempt to get to the head of the queue. Be prepared for vehicles to suddenly pull out in front of you without signalling. In big cities there are countless moped riders and their driving can be utterly unpredictable. Within cities and towns expect to see the unexpected such as; underpowered motorcycles carrying several people, small donkeys straining to pull impossibly overloaded carts, horse and pedestrian carts are also common. There will be rickety bicycles, the lunatic moped riders and all these vehicles are sharing the roads with large buses and heavy trucks. As if that was not enough to look out for, pedestrians will cross the street anywhere they like, often without looking.

When driving on major roads in rural areas shepherded animals may well be grazing the verges and you will be sharing the carriageways with donkey carts, mopeds, tractors, trucks and minibuses in varying states of roadworthiness. Drivers are prone to overtaking on bends or before hills and at other inappropriate times. At night vehicles may have defective lights, or none at all. Apart from on main roads travelling at night in rural areas should be avoided, and defensive driving practised at all times!

Morocco is a hot, dry country in summer, but during the winter mountain passes can be closed because of snow; road signs will indicate closures and, if you speak a little French, you can check on current road conditions at bus stations and Gendarmerie posts. Heavy rain is to Morocco what snow is to the south of England! Always totally unexpected and no one knows what to do or how to cope with it. Where storm water facilities are provided they are often poorly designed or badly maintained, as a result enormous puddles obscure roads, fields are turned into lakes and occasionally roads and even bridges are washed away. In the winter of 2009 parts of the Mediterranean coast road washed away and in other places were blocked by falling debris. However we saw surveyors taking measurements and various hoardings en route made promises for new yachting marinas and golf complexes alongside this narrow stretch of scenic road, so it seems likely that it will be upgraded.

Roundabouts 'Priorité à droite' - Beware, traffic entering some roundabouts has priority over traffic already on the roundabout. These roundabouts with priority to the right are more common in towns and cities. The problem is that there is no hard and fast rule, and at some you will see 'Give Way', or 'Vous n'avez pas la priorité' signs on the approach, meaning that traffic on that roundabout has priority. Our advice is that you should take particular care; it's very easy to get caught out!

TARFAYA	100	طرفـايـة
TAN-TAN	305	طانطان
GUELMIM	435	كلـمـيـم
TIZNIT	583	تيزنيت
AGADIR	640	أكـّاديـر
ESSAOUIRA	811	الصويـرة
SAFI	936	أسـفـي
EL JADIDA	1056	الجـديـدة
CASABLANCA	1152	الدارالبيضاء
RABAT	1242	الربــاط

Motorhome Servicing

There are four places in Morocco where some parts and accessories are available and repairs to the habitation equipment can be carried out:

Ets Usinag
Rue Cheikh Maa El Ainine,
Quartier Industriel,
Agadir.
Tel: 0673 794362
N30°25.460' W009°35.180'

Camping Car Service Trigano
Imi Ouadda.
Km 27 Route D'Essaouira.
Opposite the entrance to Atlantica Parc campsite.
Tel: 0678 747129
N30°35.275' W009°45.056'

Camping Car Service Trigano
Tiznit.
Towards the edge of town,
signed off the road to
Aglou Plage.
N29°42.459' W009°44.198'

Camping Car Maroc
(also hires motorhomes)
At the Camping Car Maroc campsite,
Off the N9, west of Marrakech,
signed.
Tel: 0661 95 55 17
N31°36.822' W007°53.421'
See page 105.

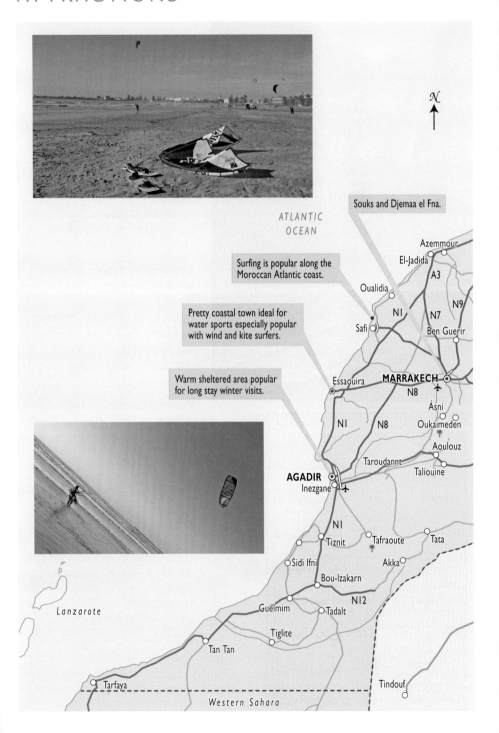

ATLANTIC OCEAN

Souks and Djemaa el Fna.

Surfing is popular along the Moroccan Atlantic coast.

Pretty coastal town ideal for water sports especially popular with wind and kite surfers.

Warm sheltered area popular for long stay winter visits.

Azemmour

El-Jadida

A3

Oualidia

N9

N1

N7

Safi

Ben Guerir

Essaouira

MARRAKECH

N8

Ásni

N1

N8

Oukaimeden

Aoulouz

Taroudannt

Taliouine

AGADIR

Inezgane

N1

Tiznit

Tafraoute

Tata

Sidi Ifni

Akka

Bou-Izakarn

N12

Lanzarote

Guelmim

Tadalt

Tiglite

Tan Tan

Tarfaya

Tindouf

Western Sahara

SPAIN

Marbella

Melilla

Algeciras   Gibraltar

Strait of Gibralta

MEDITERRANEAN SEA

Ceuta (Sebra)

Fes tannery - don't turn your nose up!

TANGER   N13

Asilah

Melilla

Al Hoceima

Saïdia

Larache

N2

Nador   N2   Ahfir

Tlémcen

Moulay Bousselham

Ketama

Targuist

Berkane

Roman ruins of Volubilis.

Ouazzane

A1

Souk-el-Arba du-Rharb

Taounate   N15   N6   **OUJDA**   N22

Sidi-Kacem

Taza   Guercif   Taourirt

N8

Kenitra   N4

Moulay Yâcoub

N6

Salé

Moulay-Idriss

FÈS

Âïn-Benimathar

RABAT

Meknès

Oued Sebou

Mohammedia

A1   N13   N8   Sefrou

N17

Ben Slimane

Ifrane

CASABLANCA

Azrou

N15

N11

Khenifra

Missour

Tendrara

Settat

Khouribga   Oued-Zem   N8

M O R O C C O

Bouârfa

Oued Oum er Rbia

Beni-Mellal   Kasba-Tadla

Midelt

Figuig

N8

Afourer

Imilchil

N13   N10   Beni Ounif

Azilal

Ar-Rachidia

Demnate

N10   Béchar

N9

Tinerhir   Erfoud

Cascades d'Ouzoud.

Skoura   Boumalne-Dadès

Oued Dadès

Taghit

Ouarzazate

Agdz   Taouz

Erg Chebbi. Large Saharan sand dune.

N10

Tazenakht   N9

Tazzarine

Zagora

Todra Gorge.

Beni Abbès

Mhamid

Gorge du Dadès.

A beautiful Palmeraie and attractive kasbah which has a campsite in its grounds.

Aït Benhaddou is a fortified city along the old caravan route from Sahara to Marrakech.

INTRODUCTION

Maps

We advise that you buy maps in the UK before you depart for Morocco. The best road map for general use in Morocco is the Michelin 742, however a few years ago the road numbering system changed and some road signs still retain the old route numbers. The Michelin 959 map (now out of print) was the last one to carry the old road numbers, if you can find a copy it could prove useful on occasions to help verify your location. The spelling of some place names in Morocco varies, to save confusion this guide conforms to the spelling on the 742 Michelin map. Road signs are generally dual language, Arabic and French. Also consider buying town maps for your tourist excursions, as the Medinas can be difficult to navigate.

Satellite Navigation GPS

It is unlikely that your standard satellite navigation, GPS, system will have adequate Moroccan mapping. Garmin Nuvi's loaded with Europe mapping have skeleton mapping for Morocco but this is insufficient for navigation. Nuvi's will show you your location in the country and will show you how far you are away from one of the sites in this guide, if you have entered the co-ordinates. At the time of writing (August 2009) Ndrive was the only 'portable navigation device' (PND) manufacturer offering mapping for Morocco see www.ndriveweb.com Their G280 costs €160 including shipping, this model is also on sale in Morocco. Existing Ndrive PND owners can download Moroccan mapping from Ndrive's website at a cost of €45. The Moroccan maps enable navigation on the entire road network. Street-level coverage is provided for Casablanca, Fez, Marrakesh, Rabat and Tangier. We understand that TomTom may supply Morocco maps but this has not been confirmed.

Speeding and Checkpoints

Fixed speed cameras are uncommon in Morocco but Police operating mobile speed checks are commonplace throughout the country. On the spot fines are issued if you are caught speeding. Speed limits are normally well signed and are generally: 40 or 50kph in built up areas, 60 or 80kph in smaller communities or at hazards, 100kph on main roads outside of towns and 120kph on the toll motorways. The Police also operate roadside driver and vehicle checks, generally motorhomes are waved through with a smile, occasionally you may be stopped and asked if everything is ok, where you have been and where you are heading. South of Tarfaya, and near the border with Algeria, there is a military presence and you will be stopped at checkpoints. You are expected to hand over a 'fiche' which is a document with the information detailed below: If you are going to these areas we recommend you prepare several copies in advance for each person.

Nom	Surname
Prénom	Forename
Date de naissance	Date of birth
Lieu de naissance	Place of birth
Nationalité	Nationality
Profession	Occupation
Domicile	Home address
Situation familiale	Marital status (single: célibataire – married: marié if male, mariée if female, divorced: divorcé/divorcée - widowed (veuf/veuve)
Nom du père	Father's name
Nom de la mère	Mother's name
Passeport no.	Passport number
Délivré le	Passport issue date
Délivré à	Passport place of issue
Valide jusqu'à	Passport expiry date
Date d'entrée Maroc	Date of entry to Morocco
Ville d'entrée	Port of entry to Morocco
No. de Police	Police number stamped in the back of your passport on entry
Motif du voyage	Purpose of visit (Tourisme)
Marque du véhicule	Vehicle make
Immatriculation	Vehicle registration number
Venant de	Coming from (town where you stayed last night)
Allant à	Going to (town where you will be staying tonight)

Fuel

Diesel and unleaded petrol are widely available, but there are no LPG Autogas stations in Morocco. Outside of towns fuel stations may be long distances apart so it is advisable to top up your tank whenever possible. Choose the well-known European brands where available, and also buy fuel from busy stations, thus reducing the risk of buying contaminated fuel. For common rail and similar modern diesel engines it is recommended that only the higher quality Gasoil 350 (now being phased out) or Gasoil 50 be used. Fuel stations are mostly open 7 days a week. Prices are fairly constant across the country, except in Western Sahara where fuel is duty free. In January 2009 standard diesel cost around 7.35Dh per litre, Gasoil 50 cost around 10.35Dh per litre.

Children Begging

Begging children are a constant problem. Whenever you stop, children seem to appear out of nowhere and soon start asking for pens, sweets, presents or money (stylo, bonbon, cadeau, Dirham). Giving anything to children is strongly discouraged; no matter how appealing, or demanding they may be. Far better, particularly in the more isolated rural areas, is to try to find out where the local school is, and donate writing or drawing materials there.

Medical

Medical facilities in the major cities are generally acceptable, but not up to European standards. Minor ailments or injuries can be dealt with satisfactorily at local clinics but for more serious problems it may be necessary to use a private clinic or hospital. Travel insurance is essential, most insurers have a helpline which should be contacted for guidance in the event of a medical problem.

INTRODUCTION

Out and About

Safety

Once you get over any initial nerves you will soon feel comfortable in Morocco. Petty crime is not a significant problem, in fact you often see shopkeepers protecting their stock with nothing more than a sheet of cloth whilst they go off for lunch! Of course, you should take the normal precautions, keeping valuables out of sight and locking them away in a safe when leaving the vehicle. Wearing a money belt under clothing is always advisable when you're out and about but especially so when you're in the souks. A fake 'muggers wallet' is another safety tool worth having wherever you travel. A muggers wallet contains expired cards and a small amount of cash that you can hand over should the need arise. At Vicarious Books office we receive more reports of handbags being stolen than any other crime. Just don't keep valuables in handbags, they are like wrapped Christmas presents to thieves.

Parking - Select places to park with care, a small payment to a 'guardian' for a parking place is obviously preferable to a scruffy looking back street but there is no guarantee that the same guardian will still be there on your return.

When guardians offer to look after your vehicle appropriate 'donations' are:

1 or 2Dh 10 minutes or less
5 Dh up to 2 hours
10 Dh all day

Religion

Morocco is a Muslim country. Modesty in clothing and affection will be expected, especially in remote areas. Pork and alcohol are not widely available, and are expensive. In Marrakech expect to pay around £5 for a 300ml beer in a tourist bar, the spectacle going on outside is thrown in for free. Non-Muslims are strictly forbidden to enter Mosques, except for a few that sell entry tickets to visitors.

Ramadan is an annual month long fast and Muslims are only supposed to eat between dusk and dawn. During Ramadan, especially outside of tourist areas, shops and restaurants may close during the day. Publicly eating and drinking during the day, especially near Mosques, will be frowned upon. The start of Ramadan is the: 22nd August 2009, 11th August 2010, and 1st August 2011.

Communication

Language - Arabic is the national language of Morocco, but the local language of Berber is sometimes heard. Being an ex French colony many Moroccans speak French as a second language, the greatest number of tourists visiting Morocco are French nationals and for these two reasons French is the main 'tourist language'. Moroccans are great linguists and it is not uncommon in tourist areas to come across people that speak many languages even Japanese! If 'vous parlez un peu français' you should start any conversation with a Moroccan in French, if they speak English they will often reply back to you in English.

Mobile Phone - Mobile coverage is good in most of the country. UK mobile phones will work in Morocco but beware, you will be charged at international rates not the cheaper European roaming rates. Check with your provider before you go! The Moroccan phone system changed from 9 digits to 10 digits on 7th March 2009, fixed-line phone numbers starting with 02 or 03 changed to 052 and 053. Phone numbers (mobiles) starting with 01, 04, 05, 06 or 07 changed to 061, 064, 065, 066 or 067, while those starting with 08 or 09 became 080 and 089. The old 9 digit numbers do not work.

There is limited, but growing, 3G-network availability and GPRS is widely available. Roaming data rates are high, being much more expensive than in Europe. If your phone is unlocked it can be cost effective to buy a readily available Moroccan pay-as-you-go SIM card. Maroc Telecom has the best mobile coverage throughout the country. Using a local SIM card means that calls within the country will be much cheaper, incoming calls will be free to you. When buying a Moroccan SIM card take your phone with you and get the shopkeeper to help you set it up. The initial menu voice prompts are in Arabic and you will need help to change them to French, the only other language available.

Emergency Numbers - The emergency phone number for Police is 19 and for Ambulance is 15. The response may be patchy and in some cases it may be more effective to seek assistance from someone familiar with local arrangements.

Internet - Cyber cafes are widely available throughout Morocco; even the smallest town will usually have one or two. Rates are very reasonable, normally around 5Dh per hour. French style keyboards have keys in different locations; thankfully most cyber cafes will accomodate your own laptop on to their network. Increasingly, campsites are offering internet access. This may simply be the use of the office computer but some campsites have dedicated computers available. WiFi, pronounced 'wee fee' in French, is available at some campsites and is often free.

Data over GPRS and 3G is not available on Maroc Telecom standard PAYG SIM cards, but you can buy a Maroc Telecom 3G PAYG SIM. This sim should work in unlocked UK USB modems (dongles) but you may need help from the shopkeeper to set it up. These are available from Maroc Telecom agencies in towns and in some Marjane supermarkets. The cost of a Maroc Telecom 3G PAYG SIM in March 2009 was 200Dh and included one-month unlimited internet usage. Top ups can be bought for periods of up to a month. You can also buy the complete package, including USB modem and one-month usage, for 800Dh. In our experience the Maroc Telecom 3G service works well in large towns, however it's not as fast as most UK 3G services, and in

rural areas we sometimes struggled even to get a GPRS connection.

Wana, a relatively new provider, also offers a PAYG 3G service but there is no Wana 3G SIM card available, so you would have to buy the Wana USB dongle, costing around 800Dh including one month usage. These are available from Wana agencies in towns and in some Marjane supermarkets. Monthly top ups from Wana cost 200Dh, for unlimited 3G access.

Both the Maroc Telecom and Wana USB modems feature automatic installation, if you buy the Maroc Telecom 3G SIM card for use in your own USB modem you will need these settings:

Maroc Telecom 3G settings:
APN: www.iamgprs2.ma
NO: * 99 #
USER: leave blank
PASSWORD: leave blank

LPG Gas

There are no LPG Autogas stations in Morocco and, as far as we know, there is no provision for refilling fixed gas tanks. Moroccan gas cylinders have the same screwed fitting as French bottles and it may be possible to get these types of cylinders refilled at gas plants in the country. We understand that refilling foreign bottles is not officially allowed and where possible costs 70Dh. Some campsites near to gas plants will offer a collect and return refill service, the refill gas is almost always butane. It may be difficult to get UK cylinders refilled due to the different fitting used. This list of gas plants may be able to refill cylinders; we offer no guarantee that any of them will actually do so!

Agadir – Zone Industriel (near the port).

Ar Rachida – N13 Midelt road.

Beni Mellal – N8 Marrakech road.

El Marsa – (Laayoune port).

Kenitra - Quartier Industriel (near the port).

Larache – Zone Industriel.

Marrakech – N7 Safi road.

Meknes – N13 Azrou road.

Mohamedia – On the R322.

Tetouan – N2 Chefchaouen road.

Tiznit – R104 Tafraout road.

Other options:

1. For short visits you may be able to take sufficient gas supplies with you, particularly if you can utilise electric hook-ups for cooking and heating.

2. For longer visits consider having your gas system adapted to take a Camping Gaz cylinder, before leaving the UK. If you like cooking outside you could buy a portable gas-cooking appliance with a Camping Gaz fitting, then buy a camping gas type cylinder in Morocco.

3. It may be possible to get UK propane cylinders refilled if you can supply an adapter to convert the outlet to the French male thread, but remember that the refill gas will probably be butane.

4. If you feel competent working with gas systems you could buy a Moroccan gas cylinder costing 200Dh full, plus a regulator and appropriate pipe work. Modern 30mB motorhome gas systems are designed so that by simply changing the pig tails different cylinders can be used. Moroccan bottles utilise the same screw fitting as French cylinders so all that may be required is to buy and attach a French pigtail Moroccan gas bottle, exchanges costs 40-50Dh.

INTRODUCTION

Money

The national currency is the Moroccan Dirham (Dh); this is not generally traded outside of the country so you may not be able to obtain any until you arrive. Exchange rates can be checked here http://themoneyconverter.com Money can be exchanged in Ceuta. At Tangier, just outside Customs there are Bureaux de Changes offices, banks and ATMs but they may not always be functioning. Most towns have branches of the main Moroccan or French banks and these often have ATMs outside where cash can be withdrawn using UK Credit or better still Debit cards. Using ATMs during bank opening hours is a good idea just in case you need help. Euros are accepted at some businesses in tourist areas and at some campsites. Credit and Debit cards are not widely accepted for payment, except in main supermarkets and at larger tourist shops. Few fuel stations accept cards and seeing a Visa sign on display does not guarantee card acceptance. Fuel stations operated by the major brands are increasingly accepting cards.

There are four notes of equal size: 200Dh is blue, 100Dh is brown, 50Dh is green, and the 20DH is purple. Coins are 10Dh, which is brass with a silver insert, 5Dh is smaller and silver with a brass insert, the 2Dh, 1Dh, 1/2Dh coins are all silver metal and step down in size inline with value. The smallest denomination coins are 20-santimats and 10-santimats, these are called 'centimes' when speaking French, and are a brassy colour metal, and step down in size inline with value.

Goods are often sold for odd prices, such as Muesli 21.15Dh or Cornflakes 9.99Dh. However there are no 5-santimat or even 1-santimat coins and amounts are usually rounded up.

Food Shopping

Main towns and cities are likely to have: Marjane, Acima or Macro supermarkets making 'civilised' shopping easy. The Country's big hypermarket chain is Marjane and the stores appear modelled on French hypermarkets. There are Marjane stores at Rabat, Agadir, Tangier, Fès, Mohammedia, Tétouan, Casablanca, Meknès, Marrakech, Oujda, Safi and Kénitra. Marjane stores are normally signed on major roads in these towns. There are a few Carrefour supermarkets along the northern coast. Metro stores are also present in the country but you need a membership card. Acima and Aswak Assalam are two other national supermarket

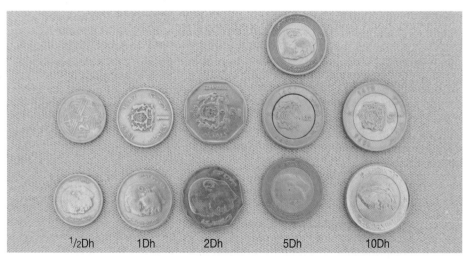

| 1/2Dh | 1Dh | 2Dh | 5Dh | 10Dh |

chains, they don't advertise as well as other brands and are more difficult to find. Also unlike Marjane they tend not to have butchery or greengrocery departments.

Small provisions shops can be found in virtually all towns and villages. Usually these are located in relatively modern arcades. Grocery stores, 'alimentares' or 'epiceries', are seldom labelled such, but are often distinguishable by YAWMY (a brand of yoghurt), KRAFT, OMO, TIDE or PEPSI advertising signs.

Most of these booth type shops have a counter across the front behind which goods are stacked floor to ceiling along the three walls. They sell: tinned goods, tomatoes, beans, pulses, fish etc. Dried goods: semolina, pulses etc. Household consumables: washing powders, washing up liquid, cloths etc. Tea (mint and other Moroccan flavours), sugar, instant coffee, biscuits, cakes, and sweets will be on sale. Processed cheese, margarine/butter, milk and processed meats (usually turkey mortadella) are available, some of these shops have refrigeration units, but most don't. They'll often sell bread (kept either in a glass case on the counter or in a sack behind it) and almost always bottled water, coca cola and other fizzy drinks often stacked in piles or crates outside the front. Few Grocers also sell greengrocery.

Greengrocers are usually obvious with their displays of fruit and vegetables spread across the pavements. Butchers tend to have animals parts hanging up at the front of the shop, cold cabinets or refrigerated units are usually located at the back. Poulterers often have a painted chicken sign out front, inside live and dead chickens are for sale, 'at least you know they're fresh', they will also sell eggs and may also sell rabbits. Turkey is the cheapest meat for sale in the country.

Chemists, called Pharmacies, are found everywhere, and are usually very well signposted. Post Offices are also well signed. Post boxes are yellow in colour and the post can be erratic. Banks are common and easily recognised. ATMs are often outside.

Large towns will have permanent souks (market areas) where almost anything can be bought from the stallholders. It is all too convenient to shop in the comfort of the supermarkets but you can do so much more for the local community and economy by buying from small shops and souks whenever possible. Remember you represent tourism and it is local people that provide most of the camping and parking facilities. Small towns will usually have a weekly souk, where locals bring their produce to sell. Ask at your campsite what day, and where, the local market is held, they are always worth visiting, if only for the experience.

Food Prices and Availability

Unlike other goods the price quoted for food is the price paid, food is not haggled. Here are the prices from March 2009:

Bread - White bread is available everywhere. Moroccan bread is round and flat and ranges from 20-30 cm in diameter. A loaf costs between 1 and 2Dh. Baguettes are available in tourist resorts and occasionally wholemeal (Complet) which is slightly more expensive.

Water - Bottled water is available everywhere at Tabacs, Epiceries etc. A litre costs between 2-2.5 Dh. Marjane supermarkets sell 5 litre bottles from 12Dh.

Milk - Fresh milk is sold in 450g sachets, semi (green) 2.95Dh, entire (blue) 3.15Dh. Milk is available from most grocery stores but is not always refrigerated. UHT milk can be bought at the larger stores (Marjane etc.) for 8.95Dh a litre.

Eggs - Eggs are 1Dh each at smaller shops, in remote areas look for a chicken sign. Eggs cost slightly more in the larger stores.

Tea - The only British style tea available is Lipton's Yellow Label. 25 teabags cost 10Dh and 100 teabags costs 45Dh at Marjane supermarkets and larger alimentaries.

Coffee - Nescafe is available in almost all stores costing 30Dh for a 100g jar.

Sugar - Sugar is available everywhere which is not surprising once you have tried mint tea. Expect to pay 5Dh for a kilogram.

Pasta - Dried pasta is widely available, a 500g pack costs 15Dh, but is cheaper in larger stores.

Margerine & Butter - Both are widely available but are seldom refrigerated. A 250g pack costs 7.90Dh.

Oranges - Approximately 6Dh a kilo.

Vegetables - When buying fruit and vegetables in a souk or a local shop you are given a bowl, usually a coloured plastic washing up bowl. You fill the bowl with fruit and vegetables of your choice. Usually everything is weighed together! And you're charged accordingly. For example in a souk 6 potatoes, 2 onions, 4 tomatoes, 1 cucumber, and 6 oranges weighs 3 kilos at 6Dh per kilo = 18Dh, small shops would charge about 10Dh per kilo for the same. Vegetable prices vary with the season and the weather.

Meat - At butchers' shops meat is cut to order. Lamb and beef costs between 75-100Dh a kilo and chickens from as little as

30Dh. It is difficult to buy pork products but Marjane supermarkets have a very small selection of bacon, ham and salami.

Fresh Fish - Along the coast fish is widely available. Enterprising fishermen will often visit campsites. Larger coastal towns will have a fish market. Inland, fish is only available at very large stores.

Fresh sardines cost approximately 15Dh a kilo and canned 4Dh.

Frozen Food - Frozen food is only available at larger stores.

Alcohol - In most Moroccan towns it is difficult to buy beer, wine or other alcohol. However you can buy alcohol at Marjane supermarkets and normally there is a limited selection of imported wines, beer and spirits. A 300ml can of Moroccan Flag beer costs 7.9Dh. Morocco produces some good wines, a bottle costs from 25Dh.

Souvenir Food Products

Dates - There are loads of date varieties and some will be on sale wherever you go. The Draa valley is the major date growing region and Medjool dates are said to be the best.

Argan Oil - Argan oil is the Moroccan equivalent of truffles. Its unique taste goes great with salads and the oil can be used like olive oil; surprisingly Argan oil is also used and sold as a toiletry. At 120Dh for 100mls Argan oil is not cheap, it can be bought from roadside stalls for less but there is a risk that it has been adulterated. There are women's co-operatives, which you can visit and buy direct from the producers. Argan trees are grown near the coast from Essaouira to Agadir.

Olive Oil - Moroccan olive oil is about the same price as oil bought in Spain. Olive oil is widely available and trees are grown in the north, High, Middle Atlas areas.

Nougat - This sweet treat is widely available but is seldom wrapped, wrapped nougat is available in supermarkets.

Saffron - This is one product that is much cheaper in Morocco than can be bought in the UK. Crocuses are grown around the Talouine area.

Eating Out

There are loads of booths, cafés and roadside stalls selling brochettes (grilled, skewered lamb or chicken), pizzas, lamb koftas and tajines (a traditional stew, slow cooked in a conical terracotta pot on charcoal). Meals from these Moroccan fast food outlets are incredibly cheap. A kofta or brochette in bread is about 20Dh and for 5Dh you can have a salade Maroccain, comprising of chopped tomatoes with onions and whatever else they have. French rule has left one sweet legacy, as fancy pastries are available in every big town.

Every dining experience is available in big towns: From street food and Pizza to restaurants serving traditional Moroccan food and others specialising in French or Italian, there are trendy bars and high-class restaurants. If you want to eat out in style and pay much less than you would in the UK visit www.bestrestaurantsmaroc.com Restaurant set meals can be a good cheap option and often comprise of a starter of Moroccan Salad, a choice of couscous or tajine followed by a fruit salad. In Essaouira at the restaurant on the corner of the square that separates the town from the fishing port it was possible to have the above three-course set-menu for

50Dh, the food was tasty and extremely good value for money.

Food worth trying: Pastilla - a pigeon pie (beware the tiny bones) from Marrakech, Mchoui - oven roasted whole lamb from Merzouga, Kefta Mkaouara - meatballs in a spicy tomato and onion sauce, sometimes including aubergines, with poached eggs floated on the top, and Salade Paysanne - a fresh salad dressed with Argan oil is sublime, and is available in the north of the country.

If you don't want to cook and you can't be bothered to go out, don't worry as many campsites have their own restaurants, not only can you eat there often they will deliver hot food to your pitch. On small family run campsites home cooked food is often available on request even if there is no restaurant.

Moroccan Tea - Tea will be offered if you visit a Moroccan's home, and often in shops. Served in small glasses, usually the brew is flavoured with fresh mint and is very sweet. Drinking tea is as much about ritual as refreshment. The tea making ceremony involves pouring the tea back and forth between pot and glass before the final pour from a height into the glass.

Don't Dabble, Haggle

Trying to buy non-essential items can be intimidating and frustrating as there are no set prices. Haggling is the accepted way of life when buying non-essential goods and any purchase can involve a long-drawn-out negotiation. It is your duty for the sake of future tourists only to pay a fair price for things but never haggle over food prices, if you feel the price for food items is too much just walk away. Before trying to buy things in the souks you should visit a government shop where everything is sold at a fixed but slightly inflated price. Write down the prices of items you are interested in, you can use this as a guide in the souks assuming goods are the same quality.

How to Haggle:

Set a price: Assess the quality and condition and work out the price you would expect to pay for such an item in England. You will probably need to visit several stalls to work out the correct price to pay but also to work out the quality available. Opening bids from stallholders could be four times more than the actual selling price.

Practice: You will not be able to browse in the souks without some friendly banter. If you show any interest in something you will be encouraged to buy, if you say you don't want it and the stallholder continues to encourage you, then this is a good opportunity to practice haggling but be careful not to buy things you just don't want.

Open negotiations: The stallholder will name a price, which will be far too high and you will react as if he is completely delusional. You will then be asked how much you are willing to pay and you state a price that is far too low and the stallholder will now look mortified (they use the guilt card a lot). Now the fun begins, but you are unlikely to be able to get to the price you want without a few trump cards.

Be careful what you say: Never display keen behaviour and never say you want or need it, after all there will be another 10 stalls selling the same thing and that 'must have' thing may be just what you don't want when you get it home. If a husband or wife is in negotiation and the other half says, "hurry up and just buy it" you might as well hand over your cheque book.

Go Quiet: Once you have made your final bid for the price you are willing to pay, stop talking and keep completely silent. The only thing left to say after a minute or so is that it was your final offer.

Walk away: During negotiations if you can't get to the right price just walk away, if the seller can go lower he will do so and you are likely to start negotiations again at a more favourable price. You can repeat this exercise several times; you will know when you have reached the true price, as the stallholder will stop chasing after you and you now have the upper hand.

Money Talks: If you know exactly what you want to buy and how much you are prepared to pay, put the money in a pocket in advance. It's hard to turn down cash in a take it or leave it situation.

Enjoy it: It is all about the experience so relax and enjoy it and don't forget that there are still another 10 stalls selling the same thing.

Souvenirs

Carpets, rugs and blankets - These are the clichéd goods to buy. There probably are bargains to be had but carpets and rugs are not low cost items. The towns of Midelt, Azrou, Asni, Chichaoua and Tinerhir have good shops. Blankets and throws will be on sale throughout Morocco with some beautiful articles displayed.

Woollen goods and fabrics - There are stunning knitted items for sale in the Essaouira area of the coast. Especially cheap are the beanie hats at 20Dh each; there are also knitted and woven jackets for sale. Keep your eyes open and you will see kids knitting in the town and surrounding villages. Berber men often wear long lengths of fine material wound around their heads; women wear similar material as scarves and shawls. There are many different colours and types of fabrics available, especially in the south. The black material embroidered with glowing coloured patterns is particularly striking. Moroccan silk is made from cactus fibres.

Upholstery and curtains - We came across two different motor-caravanners who had their motorhome upholstery re-covered whilst in Morocco. With such wonderful fabrics and cheap skilled labour available this makes perfect sense. Search out sofa and mattress makers on the main streets. Other campers had taken measurements at home and brought curtain header tape and lining material with them so that they could get

curtains made. Meknes and Marrakech have fabric souks, but so will most large towns.

Wood Products - There are beautifully carved bowls and inlaid boxes, tables and stools for sale. Unfortunately some are made from local but unsustainable timber. We particularly liked the kebab sticks made with decorated cedar wood handles sold in Marrakech.

Leather - This is another opportunity to buy very good value goods, especially bags, briefcases, sandals and babouches (slippers). Pouffes and leather coats are also widely sold and souks in larger towns will have several sellers.

Basketwork - Some interesting and mundane items are for sale: waste bins, plant pots, mats etc. Tazarine produces some good stuff but you can see wickerwork at many roadside stalls.

Henna - Henna is widely available and of course you can be decorated at almost any tourist resort.

INTRODUCTION

Minerals and Fossils - These are available all over Morocco but especially in the High Atlas and down through Erfoud. There are some beautiful things for sale, beware of fakes, particularly the brightly coloured crystals, which are often coloured artificially. Deodorant crystals are often for sale at spice stalls. Look for white almost clear soft rock; this could be mistaken for ice and apparently comes in different grades. When this mineral is added to water it dissolves until the water reaches saturation point, the resulting brine is a completely effective underarm deodorant. A spray bottle is ideal for application. Quarter fill the bottle with crystals, add water and use daily.

Pottery - Everyone says Safi is the best place to buy pottery but Chefchaouen has some lovely stuff in blue and Tamegroute has green glazed wares. Sale's pottery is often decorated with Islamic designs. Beware when buying tajine pots, as some are purely decorative and do not survive cooking temperatures. Moroccan cooking tajines are designed for slow/low cooking on charcoal, not high heat gas stoves.

Jewellery – Moroccan made jewellery is not as widely available as you'd think. Historically Jewish smiths who have now left the country made jewellery. Tiznit has a jewellery making

souk and there are some lovely coral pieces on sale in Asilah and to the north.

Brass and Copper - Not only are there some lovely old items lurking in souks (especially teapots) there is still a thriving brass and copper industry, particularly in Fez, where you can order items to your own specifications.

Apothecary Souks - Cures for almost every ailment imaginable are available. A tour of a stall is interesting and shouldn't be missed. Herbal Viagra is allegedly hard to beat!

Kohl - This is a mixture of soot and other ingredients, used by women to darken the eyelids and as mascara. Kohl is sold loose and is reasonably priced, and is particularly available in the Marrakech area.

Rose water and Attar of Roses - The area around Skoura, El Kelaa M'Gouna and Boumalne Dades specialises in rose growing and the rose fragranced water is sold all over the area. There are a couple of small factories, which you can visit but most of the petals are exported to Grasse in France, for use in the perfume industry.

Olive oil soap - Particularly sold around the Demnate area.

Vicarious Books

Sea View Camping

This unique campsite guide shows you all the sea view campsites around Great Britain. All you have to do is choose where you want to go and be ready for a fantastic time as you explore one of the most diverse coastlines in the world.

To help you make informed choices, a photo of the sea view from each inspected site is included. Descriptions are given about the sites, their facilities and amenities, especially if beach access is possible. In addition, the location of the nearest pub, shop, beach and slipway is provided to further enhance your choice. GPS Co-ordinates are included.

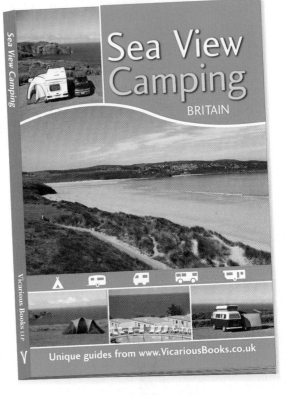

If you love being by the sea then this is the campsite guide for you.

only **£11.99** inc UK P&P

To order, give us a call or visit our website to buy online.

0131 208 3333   **www.VicariousBooks.co.uk**

CAMPING

CACTACEAE
Echinocactus grusonii
Amérique du sud

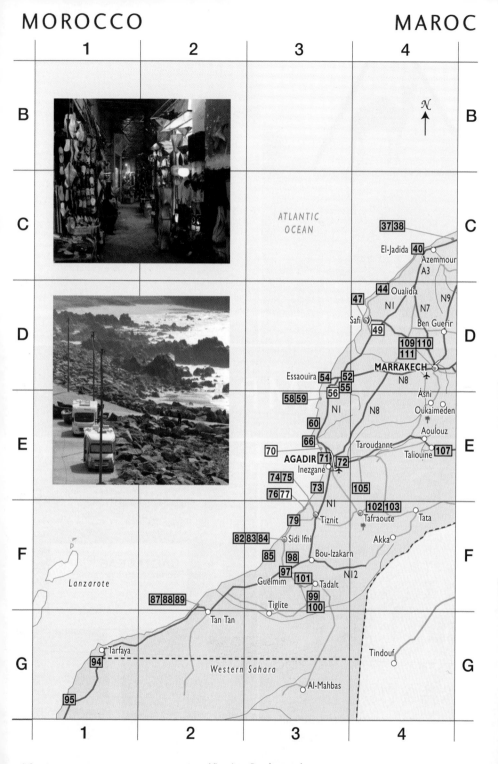

ATLANTIC
OCEAN

37 38

El-Jadida 40 Azemmour
A3

44 Oualidia
47 N1 N9
N7
Safi 49 Ben Guerir

109 110
111
MARRAKECH
N8

Essaouira 54 52
55
56 Asni
58 59 Oukaimeden
N1 N8 Aoulouz
60 Taroudannt Taliouine 107
66
70 AGADIR 71 72
Inezgane
74 75 73
76 77 105
N1
102 103
79 Tiznit Tafraoute Tata
82 83 84 Sidi Ifni Akka
85 98 Bou-Izakarn
97 N12
Guelmim 101 Tadalt
87 88 89 99
Tiglite 100
Tan Tan
Lanzarote

Tarfaya Tindouf
94
Western Sahara
95 Al-Mahbas

MAROC

MOROCCO

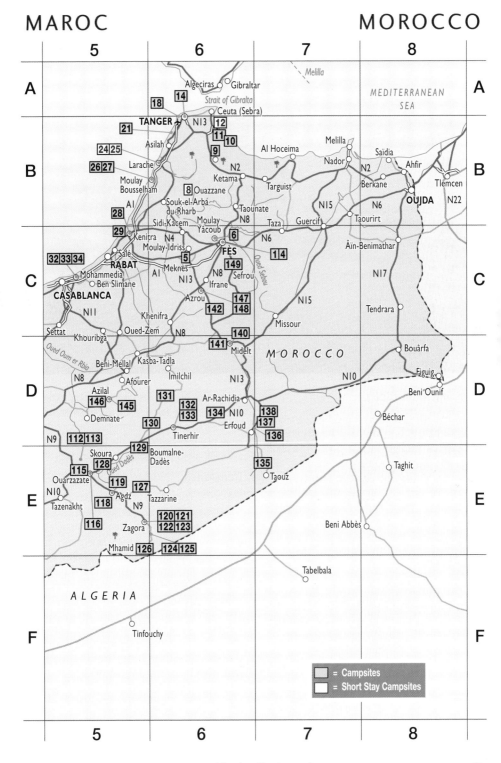

Camping in Morocco

Morocco's climate makes it great for camping, especially if you take your own vehicle and go and explore this fascinating country. The open roads and dramatic scenery will appeal to all adventurers whether they travel by bicycle, motorcycle, car, 4x4, camper or motorhome. Whatever you yearn for it is there: off road driving and dramatic snowy mountain passes, Atlantic surf and winter sun, if you want to escape for a while then head for a desert oasis.

This campsite guide is suitable for anyone going camping in Morocco, all the campsites in this guide are open all year and accessible by any form of transport. All the campsites near the coast have been inspected. A selection of campsites in the centre have also been checked, any that are a long way from main routes or tourist destinations and sites only accessible by four-wheel drive vehicles have not been included. Nearly all the campsites and parking areas in this guide are

accessible by vehicles up to 8m long. Where access is likely to be restricted to small vehicles this has been identified, in contrast sites that can accommodate large American style RV motorhomes are also identified.

Campsites

Moroccan campsites usually consist of a walled area, the ground is sometimes covered with concrete but more often is compacted sand, gravel and dirt. If there is a grassy area for tent camping it will usually be under trees. Campsite facilities vary greatly in standards and conditions. Restaurants are common but swimming pools and recreation facilities are not. Unfortunately there are few top quality campsites in Morocco, the majority of sites being some way below European standards. We have not included campsites that are very poor even by Moroccan standards!

Tent campers will need a thick sleeping mat to protect from stones and uneven ground, also pack sturdy metal pegs and a good hammer for pegging out and peg removal.

Bathroom conditions and cleanliness vary greatly from campsite to campsite. Some campsites only have continental squat toilets; others have thrones or a mixture of both. Toilet paper will not usually be provided and toilet seats will probably be absent from thrones. Showers will not necessarily be hot, or free, or even have a showerhead. Sinks are unlikely to have plugs, so a universal plug carried in your wash bag is an essential item. If you have toileting concerns ask to check the bathrooms before you book in or better still ensure you are self sufficient with your own toilet and washing facilities.

Electricity in Morocco is normally 230v 50Hz AC. Many campsites have electric hook-up facilities but few have a fully working service. The continental (French) 2-pin socket is most commonly available, but not necessarily on every pitch and then those that are available may not be in working order. When you have tracked down a functioning socket you then need a long enough cable to reach your pitch, even then you may be without electricity as supplies may be intermittent or not available at all for periods of time. When power is available it may be limited to 4Amps or less at some campsites. A few sites that are not on the main grid will have their own generator. At such campsites electricity is likely only to be available for a few hours in the evening. The good news is you will really appreciate the electricity when you get it.

Water is a precious resource in Morocco, especially in the south. Although some piped water may be indicated as 'eau potable' (drinking water) it is advised that it should all be regarded as not suitable for drinking unless you have an adequate water purifier/filter fitted. See www.aquapure.co.uk or www.generalecologyeurope.com for further information. Bottled water is readily available and relatively cheap. At some campsites there may be one or two specifically marked drinking water taps. Some of the larger campsites may have specific vehicle washing facilities, otherwise it is not generally acceptable to wash vehicles at campsites. Some sites make a charge for filling motorhome water tanks, or restrict the amount you can take.

Change is inevitable and Morocco is developing quickly yet the old ways still dominate life. Expect things to change at short notice or without notice at all. Campsite facilities may have become run down or possibly improved, sites may have closed and new ones have popped up within a few months. Please let us know by filling in one of the report forms in the back of the guide, we also need to know if things stay the same.

A separate tap for filtered water.

A fitted water filter.

FES 1 C6

Camping Diamant Vert, Km 5, Route de Aïn Chkef, Fès.
Tel: 0535 608367 www.diamantvert.ma

SP GB F D E I CC €

The campsite is located behind a holiday complex and water park but is in an attractive spot amongst large eucalyptus trees, beside a small river in the Aïn Chkef forest. Wide site roads and small pitches to one side provide motorhome places; tents pitch on the grass areas under trees. Facilities in the single sanitary block are fairly old, tired and would be inadequate if the site were busy. There is hot water to most sinks and all showers. This site is very quiet in winter and is ideal if you don't want the full facilities offered at Camping International, it is also cheaper. The water park, open only in summer, has a range of pools and water slides. There is a children's play area available all year. The site provides a good base for visiting Fès, official tour guides can be arranged at reception.

Pitch No: 100 | Water: Dh | Electric: E Amp 20Dh | Disposal Details (sanitation): MB MG

Toilets: WC No. 6 No. 6 S C | Showers: No. 6 No. 6 H Dh
All hot, inc.

Directions: 5km south of Fès in the Aïn Chkhef forest. Signed 'Diamant Vert Parc' off the A1. After turning off the A1 go past the first sign 'Camping Complexe' then turn right at the roundabout, signed, the next right turn, signed, takes you into the campsite. Beware of touts in Fès who tell you that the site is closed and offer to direct or take you to Camping International.

GPS: N33°59.176' W005°01.117'

Campsite Amenities: WiFi
Washing Machine 35Dh.
Swimming pool summer only.

Local Amenities Nearby (5km or less): M
All in Fès, 5km except gas 2km on route to Meknès. The No 17 bus to the city stops near the site entrance and charges 3Dh.

+ = 70Dh | All Year | + = 65Dh

MAROC   MOROCCO

Camping International de Fès, Route de Sefrou, Fès.
Tel: 0535 731439

GB F D E I   CC €

This large campsite is well laid out amongst trees. There is a licensed bar and international and Moroccan restaurants, which are open all year. The swimming pool is open in summer. Five sanitary blocks serve 30 pitches each; although they are not all in use during the winter. Those that were open were clean and well maintained. The campsite is a good base for visiting Fès. Bus No. 38 to the city centre picks up near the campsite entrance. Official tour guides for Fès can be arranged at reception. Some road noise.

Pitch No:	Water:			Electric:			Disposal Details (sanitation):			
150		Dh		**E**	Amp	Dh	IIIII	MB	MG	
(100)				Inc.						Use toilet

Toilets:	No.	No.				Showers:	No.	No.		
WC	♂ 25	♀ 25	S	C			♂ 25	♀ 25	H	Dh

Directions: Adjacent to the R503 Sefrou road. Located 3km from Fès, right next to the big stadium. Coming from Fès turn left into the campsite just after the stadium. No signs in January 2009 possibly because of road works.

GPS: N33°59.986' W004°58.165'

Campsite Amenities:	Local Amenities Nearby (5km or less):
Laundry Service 50Dh.	All 2km on outskirts of Fès.

🚐+♂♀= 110Dh   **All Year**   ⛺+♂♀= 110Dh

Recommended routes - Route 1: From the North. Head straight into the city, following the blue signs for the Fès - Rabat motorway, eventually crossing a large roundabout into Avenue Benghazi. Pass the Place Administrative on your left (there is a sign for Hotel de Ville), in front you will see the green dome of the Municipal Theatre, go straight across into Avenue Bir Anzarane. Then, 3.5 km from the Place Administrative, at the 3rd set of traffic lights, turn right. Now follow Route A.

Route 2: From South, West or East. From the roundabout on the southern bypass (N6) where the N13 from Ar Rachida, Midelt and Azrou crosses, head into Meknès. At the 3rd set of traffic lights, in 3.9km, turn left, then follow Route A.

ROUTE A: Follow this road, with the old city walls on your left, for 2.3km, then, just after a right hand bend, turn left at a mini roundabout through the double arches (pic 1), then immediately left through more arches (pic 2). Cross the square, passing through the arches on the opposite side (pic 3). Follow this road, between the walls, turning left through an arch (pic 4) a little before the end. The campsite gates are opposite you on the right.

WARNING: Some of the archways are low, most motorhomes will not have a problem, (pic 5) shows the lowest arch, but if you are concerned follow Route 3.

Route 3: From the N6/N13 southern ring road roundabout head west to the next roundabout, where the Marjane supermarket is located. Head into Meknès and turn right at the 3rd set of traffic lights (3.3km from the roundabout). Then, at the 2nd set of traffic lights, turn left into Zenkat Maarakat Lehri, signed Palais Royale. Pass the Royal Military Academy on your right, head straight on through the arch and turn sharp right into the campsite.

Note: Routes 1 & 2 provide one of the most impressive entries to a campsite you are likely to find. If you get lost in the city just follow signs to Marjane (all over the city) and follow Route 3 from there.

GPS: N33°52.866' W005°33.371'

MAROC   MOROCCO

Camping Agdal, Meknès.
Tel: 0665 217907

Ideally situated right next to the ancient Ville Imperial. This campsite has an uncertain future, with the result that little or no maintenance has been carried out for some years and the facilities are in a poor state. This, combined with a lack of interest in keeping the facilities clean, means that what could be a very attractive site, with its tall eucalyptus trees, falls far short of what the city deserves. Concrete hard standings are located between the site roads and most require the use of levelling blocks, there is a central drain for waste water. Level shaded places are available on grass between the trees. Many electric points are in a state of disrepair and a long lead may be required to reach one that works. Meknès is a good introduction to a Moroccan city, the medina being relatively compact and hassle free.
A petit taxi from the site to the Place el Hadim in the middle of the old city is 10Dh or 15Dh after 8pm.

Pitch No:	Water:		Electric:		Disposal Details (sanitation):			
100 (100)	⚗	20Dh	**E** Amp	30Dh	⬛,	MB	MG	🔲

Toilets:	No.	No.		Showers: No.	No.		
WC	👤 10	👤 10	C	👤 5	👤 5	H ❄	7Dh

1 male and 1 female hot.

Directions: The site is difficult to find; see opposite.

Campsite Amenities:
Cold sinks only. Shop; souvenirs only, bread can be ordered.

Local Amenities Nearby (5km or less):
All 2km in City.

🚐+👤👤= 54Dh   **All Year**   ⛺+👤👤= 44Dh

MOROCCO   MAROC

Camping Bellevue, Route Moulay Idriss - Zerhoun.
Tel: 0663 569856

GB F

Very convenient for a visit to Volubilis, the best Roman site in Morocco. A small campsite on three levels, the upper part has gravel pitches for motorhomes, the middle part is terraced for tents, the lower part, with the reception, pool and sanitary facilities, has a few grass pitches to the rear for motorhomes. Trees provide shade for most of the site. Separate male and female facilities were clean and relatively well kept.

Pitch No:	Water:			Electric:			Disposal Details (sanitation):				
20 (20)	🚰	✕	Dh	E	Amp	Dh	▥	MB	MG	🔲	▦

Toilets:	No.	No.			Showers:	No.	No.		
WC	🚹 4	🚺 4	S	C ♿	🚿	🚹 4	🚺 4	H	Dh

Directions: Just off the road from Moulay Idriss to Meknès about 4km from Volubilis heading towards Meknès.

GPS: N34°00.917' W005°33.741'

Campsite Amenities:

🔲 🛁 🛒 ⚓ ✕ ⓘ WiFi

Swimming pool and restaurant summer only.

Local Amenities Nearby (5km or less):

🏋 ✕ 🛒 🏛 🚍 M 🏰 ⌀ ≈ ⌕ ⚓ 🚐 🚌

Tourist attractions 4km.

CHEFCHAOUEN 9 C6

Camping Azilan, Rue Sidi Abel Hamid, Chefchaouen.
Tel: 0539 986979 www.campingchefchaouen.com

SP GB F D E I CC €

This campsite is well situated high above the old part of town, close to the Hotel Atlas Chaouen. A flat area accommodates 30 motorhomes but there are no pitch markers. Tents are pitched on terraces in the pinewoods above. The facilities, though old, were well maintained and kept clean. The site is ideally placed for a visit to the stunningly atmospheric blue town of Chefchaouen. There is a footpath down the steep hill direct to the old part of town, alternatively you can ask the campsite reception to order a petit taxi to take you to town for 20Dh.

Pitch No: NA 30 (100) | Water: 10Dh | Electric: E 16 Amp 10Dh | Disposal Details (sanitation): MB MG

Toilets: WC No. 5 No. 5 S C | Showers: No. 10 No. 10 H 10Dh

Directions: The site is well-signed and about 2 km from the centre of the town, on the Rue Sidi Abel Hamid. Follow the signs to 'Centre Ville', 'Hotel Atlas Chaouen', then the Camping signs. The campsite is opposite the Hotel Atlas Chaouen and next to the Auberge de Jeunesse (Youth hostel). We recommend approaching from the North to avoid driving through town.

GPS: N35°10.748' W005°15.957'

Campsite Amenities: WiFi
Washing machine 30Dh. Internet available 10Dh/hr.

Local Amenities Nearby (5km or less): M
All in Chefchaouen 500m walk. Local Fair in January.

+ = 75Dh **All Year** + = 55Dh

Camping Oued Laou.
Tel: 0677 423161

This unkempt campsite is located in an olive grove. There is room for a few motorhomes on hard standing near the reception. The site is in the centre of a rather run down town and continues the theme, it could be very attractive but is sadly neglected. The three sanitary blocks appear relatively new but were un-maintained and dirty. Many electric points were broken. The town has provisions shops. Grand taxis and the bus to Tetouan leave from the centre of town. A large souk is held every Saturday about 4km out of town on the road to Chefchaouen and the surrounding area becomes chaotic. If you want to visit the souk we recommend that you take a grand taxi from the town.

Pitch No:	Water:		Electric:		Disposal Details (sanitation):	
60	5Dh		E Amp	5Dh		Use toilet
	5Dh to fill tank.					

Toilets:	No.	No.			Showers:	No.	No.	
WC	♂ 42	♀ 42	S	C		♂ 36	♀ 36	
					All cold.			

Directions: Near the centre of the town alongside the road to the beach. If coming from Tetouan continue to the end of the seafront road then turn right, site is around 100m on left. If coming from Chefchaouen the site is about 4km after the turning to Bou Ahmed. The road from Tetouan, and on to Chefchaouen was in poor condition in January 2009.

GPS: N35°26.991' W005°05.665'

Campsite Amenities:	Local Amenities Nearby (5km or less):
Cold sinks only.	Market (souk) 4km, otherwise all in town.

🚐+♂♀= 44Dh   **All Year**   ⛺+♂♀= 44Dh

MARTIL ⌖ 🏢 | **11** | **B6**

Complexe Touristique Al Boustane, BP 727, Tetouan Principal.
Tel: 0539 688822

⛺ 🚐 🚍 🚛 🚌 🚎

🚐 🚐 ⑂ ▓ SP ⚑ ▮ ♪ **GB F** D E I **CC €**

This campsite is conveniently situated as a first or last stop in Morocco. Located in the seaside resort town of Martil the campsite is 300m from the sea behind a block of flats. Pitches are marked by trees, which give some shade. The surface is mainly grass and gravel but hard standing is available on the site roadways if required. The site is well looked after, there are separate male & female sanitary blocks which are clean, hot showers are included in the price but the showerheads were missing. The swimming pool is only available in summer but the attractive onsite restaurant is open all year and serves good, reasonably priced Moroccan and European food. The town of Martil has banks, shops and a cyber cafe. There is a Marjane supermarket on the N13 close to Tetouan.

Pitch No:	Water:		Electric:		Disposal Details (sanitation):				
90	🚰	Dh	**E**	Amp **20Dh**	IIII,	MB	MG	⚑	🚌

Toilets:	No.	No.				Showers:	No.	No.		
WC	🚹 12	🚺 8	S	**C**	♿	🚿	🚹 12	🚺 10	**H**	Dh

1 disabled shower/toilet in each block.

Directions: Coming from Ceuta towards Tetouan on the N13, turn off left after M'Diq, signed 'Martil'. Follow signs for Martil then at the start of the town turn off left onto dual carriageway, signed for 'Camping Alboustane'. Carry on along this road, which turns to run along the sea front, and then turn off right when you see the sign for the campsite. The site is in about 300m on the left.
GPS: N35°37.737' W005°16.664'

Campsite Amenities: | Local Amenities Nearby (5km or less):
🔲 🛋️ 🎣 ⚔️ ⓘ Wifi | 🛒 ⚔️ 🛒 🏛️ 🚉 M 🏙️ ✏️ 〰️ 🔍 ⚓ 🎡 🚌
 | All within 1km in Martil.

🚐+🚹🚺= 65Dh | **All Year** | ⛺+🚹🚺= 60Dh

Camping Miramonte, Marchane 9000, Tanger.
Tel: 0539 937133 www.campingmiramonte.com

🏕️ 🚐 🚐 🚐 🚌 🚐

🚐 🚐 〰️ ▦ `SP` 🏴 🎵 GB F D E I CC €

This hillside campsite has several terraced areas with access for motorhomes, and grassed terraces for tents. Mature eucalyptus, pine and palm trees make this an attractive, well-shaded location. Some of the facilities show signs of neglect and were not particularly clean. There are two family bathrooms with a hot shower, toilet and basin in a separate block which were in good condition and clean. The onsite restaurant is open every evening. A swimming pool is open to the public during the summer only. These are both located almost at the top of the site up a steep hill.

Pitch No:	Water:		Electric:			Disposal Details (sanitation):				
30 (40)	🚰 ✖	**5Dh**	**E** Amp		**25Dh**	〽	MB	MG	🚽	🚌

Toilets:	No.	No.			Showers:	No.	No.		
WC	🚹 2	🚺 3	**S** C	♿	🚿	🚹 3	🚺 3	**H** ❄️	**15Dh**
					Charge for hot showers.				

Directions: Was difficult to find due to lack of signs in the town and road construction projects in the area. A new road will run west around the coast from the port. It is planned to join up with the Rabat road and is due for completion in 2009. This road, which was partly open in March 2009, goes right past the site access road and will make finding the site much easier. Access to the site may be difficult for large motorhomes because of sharp bends on the steep access road.
GPS: N35°47.663' W005°49.967'

Campsite Amenities:	Local Amenities Nearby (5km or less):
🔘 🏢 🏘 ⚓ ✖ ⓘ WiFi	🎣 ✖ 🛒 🏛 〰 M 🏰 🚣 〰 🔍 ⛺ 🚲 🚌
Washing machine 35Dh.	All within 2km in Tanger.
Swimming pool summer only.	

🚐 + 🚹🚺 = **70Dh**   **All Year**   🏕️ + 🚹🚺 = **66Dh**

CAP SPARTEL ⤵ 🔔 | 18 | A6

Camping Achakkar
Tel: 0539 333840

🏕 🚐 🚌 🚙 🚎 🚐

🚐 🚐 ⛲ ▦ SP ⚑ 🔋 🎵 **GB F D E I** CC €

A nicely situated campsite that was virtually unoccupied when visited in January. Shaded with trees, individual pitches vary in size and are marked out with hedges and shrubs. Facilities are clean and tidy and consist of two sanitation blocks with unisex showers and toilets. There is no hot water but hot showers in the bungalows may be used at a cost of 20Dh. There is no specific provision for emptying motorhome waste tanks but it may be possible to lift a manhole, check with reception. The site is right next to the cave formations called the Grottes d'Hercule and a short distance from the small Roman site of Cotta. There is guarded daytime parking and a surfing beach 2km further on towards Cap Spartel.

Pitch No:	Water:		Electric:			Disposal Details (sanitation):				
60	🔧 Inc.	Dh	E	Amp	25Dh	🚽	MB	MG	🚪	🚌

Toilets:	No.	No.				Showers:	No.	No.		
WC	🚻 6	🚻 6	S	C		🚿	🚻 6	🚻 6	H ❄	20Dh
Unisex toilets.						Unisex cold. Hot 20Dh in bungalows.				

Directions: Located 16km from the centre of Tanger. From Tanger take the N1 towards Rabat, after passing the big stadium (under construction) on the right take the next right, signed 'Cap Spartel', at the next roundabout turn left signed 'Cap Spartel'. The site is on the right in a few km, next to the entrance of Grottes d'Hercule and opposite the Hotel Le Mirage.
GPS: N35°45.553' W005°56.247'

Campsite Amenities:

🔲 🛒 🍴 ❌ ⓘ WiFi

Cold sinks only.

Local Amenities Nearby (5km or less):

🛒 ❌ 🛒 🏪 🏧 🅿 🏰 🎣 〰 🏖 🚌

Provisions 500m at Grotte d'Hercule,tourist attraction. Day parking and surf beach 2km towards Cap Spartel. Camel trips 2km towards Cap Spartel. Public transport opp. site entrance.

🚐+🚻= 85Dh | **All Year** | 🏕+🚻= 60Dh

ASILAH ⚓ 🌳   **21**   B6

Asilah Hotel Village Touristique de Briech, Briech, Asilah.
Tel: 0539 416358

Summer holiday resort hotel complex with camping fields attached. The site caters mainly for the Moroccan summer holiday visitors and little attempt is made to welcome motorhomes. The swimming pool is available in the summer. Toilets and showers are modern but were not particularly clean. Hot showers are available in the hotel on request.

Pitch No:	Water:			Electric:			Disposal Details (sanitation):				
50	♿	✂	Dh	**E**	Amp	Dh	IIII	MB	MG		

Toilets:	No.	No.				Showers:	No.		No.			
WC	♂8	♂8	S	**C**	♿	☂	♂6		♂6	**H**	❄	**10Dh**
All unisex.						6 cold, unisex. Hot 10Dh, in a hotel room.						

Directions: On the N1 coast road about 5km north of Asilah.

GPS: N35°31.926' W005°59.920'

Campsite Amenities:	Local Amenities Nearby (5km or less):
🔲 ♨ ⛏ ⚓ ✗ ⓘ Wifi	☕ ✗ 🛒 🏠 🚂 M 🏰 / ≋ 🔍 🛶 🚲 🚌
Cold water sinks.	All 5km in Asilah.

🚐+♂♀= 100Dh   **All Year**   ⛺+♂♀= 100Dh

MOULAY BOUSSELHAM 26 B6

Camping Flamants Loisirs, Moulay Bousselham.
Tel: 0537 432539 http://flamants-loisirs.ifrance.com

SP GB F D E I CC €

A large campsite shaded by eucalyptus and pine trees. A selection of large and small hard standing pitches are laid out as bays along the site roads, there is also room for around 100 tents under the trees. Pitches are well served with electric points and water taps. From a few pitches there is a view over the lagoon. Facilities are fair. Male and female blocks have communal cold showers and two hot shower cubicles each. There is disabled access to one shower/toilet.

Pitch No: 50 (100)

Water: Dh

Electric: E Amp Dh

Disposal Details (sanitation): MB MG

Toilets: WC No. 4 No. 4 S C

Disabled access to one shower/toilet.

Showers: No. 2 No. 2 H Dh

Directions: Take the 'Moulay Bousselham' exit off the motorway. Just on entering the town take the track on the left, signed for campsite. The site is about 300m. Note that the P4214 coastal road is in a very poor state and is not recommended!

GPS: N34°52.744' W006°16.820'

Campsite Amenities: WiFi

Shop, swimming pool, WiFi and restaurant summer only.

Local Amenities Nearby (5km or less): M

All 1km in the town.

+ = 90Dh **All Year** + = 90Dh

Camping Caravanning International, Moulay Bousselham.
Tel: 0537 432477

This is a very large grassy campsite in an excellent location right on the edge of the lagoon, a flamingo nesting site, and next to the small fishing port. Camping is possible within a few metres of the water or in the shade of the trees. This formerly run down site is being refurbished. The main sanitary block had been refitted with new showers and toilets, which were kept very clean. The older blocks in other parts of the site are pretty run down and were not in use when we visited in March 2009. The electricity supply was rudimentary to say the least, but new cables were being laid so this should improve. Motorhome grey and black water disposal is via a manhole alongside the first sanitary block, cassette emptying is via a screw capped drain adjacent to but not in the toilets! Meals are available to order. Boat hire is possible from 100Dh.

Pitch No:	Water:	Electric:	Disposal Details (sanitation):
500	🚰 Dh Drinking where indicated.	**E** Amp Dh	IIIII, MB MG ⌂ 🚌

Toilets:	No.	No.	Showers:	No.	No.
WC ♂4 ♀4 **S** C ♿ Unisex.			🚿 ♂4 ♀4 **H** ❄ Dh Unisex, hot in the new block.		

Directions: Take the 'Moulay Bousselham' exit off the motorway. On entering the town drive past the track on the left to Camping Flamants Loisirs. In 400m turn left, the campsite is on the left in 400m, just before the port entrance. Note that the P4214 coastal road is in a very poor state and is not recommended!
GPS: N34°52.743' W006°17.320'

Campsite Amenities:	Local Amenities Nearby (5km or less):
 Cold water sinks. Shop & swimmiing pool summer only.	 All 500m in the town.

🚐+♂♀= 70Dh   **All Year**   ⛺+♂♀= 60Dh

KENITRA 28 C5

Complexe Touristique la Chenaie, Charia el Riyada, Kenitra.
Tel: 0537 363001

SP GB F D E I CC €

This campsite is a haven away from the busy town. Some pitches are on hard standing and the remainder are on grass under pine trees. Facilities are adequate and clean. There is a restaurant and licensed bar which reputedly is busy with Moroccans in the evenings. Motorhome grey and black water disposal is via a lift up plate in front of the reception.

Pitch No:	Water:	Electric:	Disposal Details (sanitation):
150	Dh	E Amp 15Dh	MB MG

Toilets:	No.	No.			Showers:	No.	No.		
WC	3	3	S	C		4	4	H	10Dh

Directions: From the motorway take the Kenitra 'Centre' exit towards Kenitra, cross the Marjane roundabout and go straight over the next roundabout. Pass the Kenitra Polyclinique on the left then take the next turning on the right. The campsite is on the right in about 1km behind a stand of eucalyptus trees.

GPS: N34°15.575' W006°34.046'

Campsite Amenities:

WiFi

Cold sinks only. Swimming pool summer only.

Local Amenities Nearby (5km or less):

M

Provisions, restaurant, bank and public transport 1km in town. Supermarket 2km. Market (souk) 500m, daily.

+ = 35Dh | All Year | + = 28Dh

MEHDIA ⚓ 🏢 `29` C5

Camping International Mehdia Plage, Mehdia Plage, Kenitra.
Tel: 0676 896319

🏕 🚐 🚙 �car 🚌 🚐

🚐 🚐 〰 ▦ SP ▷ 🔔 △ ♫   GB F D E I CC €

This large municipal camping site has suffered from lack of investment and maintenance and there is a general air of neglect. The facilities are in a poor state but seem to be kept relatively clean. Pitches are individual hard standings. Large motorhomes can park on the site roads. This popular Moroccan summer holiday resort has a quiet and relaxed atmosphere in the winter.

Pitch No:	Water:			Electric:			Disposal Details (sanitation):				
NA 500	⚗	✗	Dh	E	Amp	20Dh	▥	MB	MG	🔟	▦

Toilets:	No.	No.				Showers:	No.	No.		
WC	♂ 18	♀ 18	S	C	♿	🚿 ♂ 18	♀ 18	H	❄	10Dh
3 blocks.						3 blocks.				

Directions: Turn off the N1 where signed for 'Mehdia Plage', just south of Kenitra. The site is in the northern part of the town, on the beach side of the main road just opposite the turning for the Gendarmerie.

GPS: N34°15.711' W006°40.447'

Campsite Amenities:
📷 ⛽ 🏪 ✗ ⓘ WiFi
Cold water sinks. Shop and restaurant summer only.

Local Amenities Nearby (5km or less):
🎣 ✗ 🛒 🏛 🚉 M 🏧 〰 ≋ Q 🛶 ⛴ 🚌
Provisions, restaurant and supermarket all 400m in town. Day parking and surf beach 200m.

🚐+♂♀= 50Dh   **All Year**   △+♂♀= 40Dh

MAROC   MOROCCO

Camping Océan Bleu, El Mansouria, Mohammedia.
Tel: 0523 311639

⛺ 🚐 🚙 🚐 🚌 🚎

🔌 🔌 ▦ ▦ SP ▷ 🜂 ♫   **GB F D E**   **CC €**

Compact family run campsite, completely walled in and shaded by eucalyptus trees and it's right opposite the beach. Facilities are somewhat rustic, but were being renovated. The owner is a charming man who speaks English well and is keen to converse. Although the onsite shop and restaurant are only open in summer, it is possible to order basic supplies and family prepared meals at reception. The use of the office computer is offered, free of charge, for internet access, WiFi is planned for the future. Gas bottle refilling (butane & propane) can be arranged, but probably not for UK bottles unless you have a French adapter. The site is a popular one night stop on the way north or south. Manoeuvring on site may be difficult for motorhomes over 8m long.

Pitch No:	Water:		Electric:		Disposal Details (sanitation):				
80	🜄 ✗ Dh		**E** Amp	**20-30Dh**	▥	MB	MG	⌐	
	Drinking water from specified taps (ask).								

Toilets:	No.	No.			Showers:	No.	No.		
WC	🚹 14	🚺 14	**C**	♿	🚿	🚹 12	🚺 12	**H** ❄	**10Dh**
					Hot available.				

Directions: On the R322, coming from Rabat around 5km before Mohammedia turn right just after police post, signed 'Camping L'Océan Bleu 800m'. Follow this rough track to the right around the dwellings and then along the coast to the left and the campsite is on the left. From Mohammedia continue on past Camping Les Mimosas down a very rough track to the campsite.
GPS: N33°44.428' W007°19.463'

Campsite Amenities:	Local Amenities Nearby (5km or less):
🗑 ⛽ 🛒 ✗ ⓘ WC	🛒 ✗ 🍴 🏛 M 🚿 🌊 Q 🚣
Washing machine 30Dh.	All around 5km in Mohammedia. Beaches opposite.

Camping les Mimosas, Plage Tilial, Pont Blondin, Mohammedia.
Tel: 0523 323325

This is a large campsite that is partly occupied by Moroccan holiday cabins. At the time of inspection large trees were being cut down and removed and the site appeared to be somewhat run-down with little evidence of cleaning or maintenance. There are 4 sanitary blocks that only had cold water but there is one male and one female sanitary block with hot water. Separate taps for drinking water are marked. A motorhome waste dump and cassette emptying point are planned.

Pitch No:	Water:		Electric:			Disposal Details (sanitation):				
200	Drinking water taps marked.	Dh	**E**	Amp	**20Dh**		MB	MG	In toilets	

Toilets:	No.	No.				Showers:	No.	No.			
WC	†36	†36	S	C			†28	†28	H	※	**20Dh**

3 male and 3 female hot, hot 20Dh.

Directions: On the R322, coming from Rabat around 4km before Mohammedia, turn right just after the Afriquia fuel station, signed 'Mimosas Beach Club'. Take next left to access the site, just before the end of the road.

GPS: N33°43.710' W007°20.214'

Campsite Amenities:

Cold water sinks.

Local Amenities Nearby (5km or less):

All around 4km in Mohammedia. Beaches 100m.

+ †† = 44Dh   **All Year**   + †† = 44Dh

MOHAMMEDIA   `34`   C5

Camping Saïd, Plage Tilial, No 120, Pont Blondin, Mohammedia.
Tel: 0523 323451

GB F D E I   CC €

A small campsite run by the Saïd family, who are most welcoming, the son and daughter both speak a little English. This rustic site and its facilities are well kept. Some shade is available. Home cooked meals can be prepared on request. They can be delivered to your motorhome or to the small room that serves as a lounge and restaurant. The camping tariff is reduced for stays of more than one night. A café and shop are both situated at the site entrance but only open in summer.

Pitch No:	Water:	Electric:		Disposal Details (sanitation):				
23	Drinking water taps marked.	E Amp 20Dh		IIII,	MB	MG		

Toilets:	No.	No.			Showers:	No.	No.	
WC	6	4	S C		Unisex, 1 hot.	H	❄	10Dh

Directions: Route R322, coming from Rabat, about 3km before Mohammedia, turn right just after new development Beverly House, signed 'Camping Saïd'.

GPS: N33°43.674' W007°20.232'

Campsite Amenities:	Local Amenities Nearby (5km or less):
Washing machine 30Dh. Internet 10Dh/hr.	All around 3km in Mohammedia. M

🚐+↑↟= 57Dh   **All Year**   **⛺+↑↟= 50Dh**

DAR BOUAZZA ⚓🏭 `37` C4

Camping International L'Oasis, Dar Bouazza, Casablanca.
Tel: 0522 221524

⛺ 🚐 🚍 🚚 🚌

⊞ ⊞ 🌾 ▦ SP ▷ 🔋 ⚱ 🎵 **GB F D E I** CC €

This campsite is virtually all covered with tarmac hard standing except for small grass tenting areas. Small trees mark the pitches but offer little shade. The pool, shop and restaurant are only open in summer. There are two sanitary blocks, one was locked at the time of inspection, hot water is generated by solar panels so may be in short supply in winter. This site is useful as a service stop or for a base to visit Casablanca. Buses and grand taxis pick up at the top of the road, or reception can arrange transport and a guide for a group of people. Drinking water is only available at the three taps adjacent to the reception.

Pitch No:	Water:	Electric:	Disposal Details (sanitation):
130	🚰 🚿 Dh Drinking water at specified taps.	E Amp 20Dh	🎚 MB MG 🚽 🚌

Toilets:	No.	No.		Showers: No.	No.			
WC	🚹9	🚺9	S C ♿	🚿 🚹11	🚺11	H ❄		15Dh

6 male and female cold. 5 male and female hot.

Directions: Just off the R320 coast road. From Casablanca take the A3 auto route, after the payage take the next exit signed 'Had Soualem', take the road towards Casablanca, then turn left by the Afriquia fuel station signed 'Dar Bouazza', carry straight on, then at the R320 turn left signed 'Azemour', site is on the right just after passing a Shell fuel station.

GPS: N33°30.369' W007°50.519'

Campsite Amenities: 🔲 🛁 🚰 ⚲ ✕ ⓘ WiFi

Local Amenities Nearby (5km or less): 🛒 ✕ 🛒 🏛 🚉 M 🏭 🌿 ≈ 🔍 🏖 🚗 🚌
All 2 km in Dar Bouazza.

🚐+🚹🚺= 75Dh   **All Year**   ⛺+🚹🚺= 60Dh

DAR BOUAZZA 38   C4

Camping International Hawaii, Dar Bouazza, Casablanca.

A large campsite with swimming pools, tennis and football pitches that are open in the summer only. The site was unoccupied and the gates locked at the time of our visit but a guardian arrived and we were assured it was open. There is hard standing parking but the facilities were in a deplorable state, not having been cleaned for some considerable time. This site should only be used as a last resort.

Pitch No:	Water:	Electric:	Disposal Details (sanitation):
60	Drinking water at specified taps.	**E** 5Dh	In toilets.

Toilets:	No.	No.	Showers:	No.	No.
WC	♠ 6	♣ 6	C	♠ 4	♣ 4

Directions: Off the R320, heading towards Azemmour, about 8km beyond Dar Bouazza take the narrow road towards the sea just before 'Mavi' signed 'Camping Hawaii', site in about 1km.

GPS: N33°28.768' W007°54.184'

Campsite Amenities:

Cold water sinks. Swimming pool and restaurant summer only.

Local Amenities Nearby (5km or less):

Small shop nearby. Beach 500m.

🚐+♠♣= 50Dh   **All Year**   **⛺+♠♣= 50Dh**

EL JADIDA   🖎 🏘 🏛 **40**   C4

Camping Caravanning International, 1, Avenue des Nations Unies, El Jadida.
Tel: 0523 342755

Å 🚐 🚎 🚐 🚌 🚐

🚐 🚐 🏮 📷 SP ⚑ 🔋 🛢 🎵   GB F D E I   CC €

This is a busy campsite. Eucalyptus trees provide some shade. Pitches are unmarked and the popularity of the site can cause units to be uncomfortably close together at times. There is a bar, restaurant and small provisions shop onsite. The bar is used mainly by Moroccans in the evening and is not welcoming. Sadly there is a general lack of care evident around the site and facilities are dirty and badly maintained. This neglect spoils what could be a very pleasant site. It is however a useful base for visiting this thriving seaside town with its old Cité Portugaise.

Pitch No:	Water:			Electric:			Disposal Details (sanitation):			
120	🚰	🚿 Dh		E	Amp	20Dh	▥	MB	MG 🗑	🚐
							Roadside drain. Toilet disposal direct to drains via lift up steel covers			

Toilets:	No.	No.				Showers:	No.	No.			
WC	🚹 12	🚺 12	S	C	♿	🚿	🚹 6	🚺 6	H	❄	5Dh

Directions: On the coast road, coming from Casablanca turn left on entering the town, signed 'Camping International'. Site is about 500m on left. From El Jadida take Casablanca road and turn right near the edge of town just after the Afriquia fuel station.

GPS: N33°14.574' W008°29.245'

Campsite Amenities:	Local Amenities Nearby (5km or less):
🔲 🍴 🛖 🏊 ✕ ⓘ WiFi	🍴 ✕ 🛒 🏠 🏛 M 🏰 🌿 ≋ 🔍 🛝 🚐 🚌
Cold water sinks.	All around 1km in El Jadida.

🚐+🚹🚺= 55Dh   **All Year**   Å+🚹🚺= 53Dh

OUALIDIA   44   D4

Camping les Sables D'Or.

🏕 🚐 🚚 🚙 🚌

🚐 🚐 ▨▨ ▦ SP ▨ 🔋 ♪ **GB F** D E I CC €

An absolutely dilapidated campsite, the facilities are in a state of disrepair and dirty. Much of the site was flooded and unusable when we visited. The only reasons to stay would be to take advantage of the partial security offered or for a service stop. The village is a Moroccan summer holiday resort and is very quiet in winter.

Pitch No:	Water:	No.	Electric:	Amp	Dh	Disposal Details (sanitation):				
100	🚰	Dh	**E** Inc.				MB	MG	🚽	

Toilets:	No.	No.				Showers:	No.	No.		
WC	👨 3	👩 3	**S**	**C**	♿	🚿	👨 3	👩 3	**H**	❄ 6Dh

Directions: Easiest access is from the road that branches off the R301 and runs towards the coast from just outside the southern most edge of the town. Follow this road and turn left at the bottom, site is on the left in a few hundred metres.

GPS: N32°44.140' W009°02.556'

Campsite Amenities:	Local Amenities Nearby (5km or less):
🗑 🛁 ♿ ✂ ⓘ WiFi	🛒 ✕ 🛒 🏛 ▦ **M** 🏙 🚿 ≈ 🔍 ⚓ 🏘 🚌
Cold water sinks.	Market (souk) Sunday. Beaches within 500m.

MOROCCO   MAROC

Camping International de Safi, Route de Mzoughen, Quartier de Sidi Bouzid, Safi 46000. Tel: 0524 463816

GB F D E I   CC €

An attractive, well kept campsite on the edge of town. Pitches are spread over various levels, mostly shaded by pine trees, facilities are well maintained and clean. Access to the ground level wastewater disposal may be difficult for large motorhomes and for all motorhomes in wet weather. There is an Internet café and provisions shop nearby. This site makes a useful base for visiting the Safi potteries and ceramics museum, a taxi into town costs around 7Dh.

Pitch No:	Water:		Electric:			Disposal Details (sanitation):				
60		Dh	E	Amp	20Dh	IIII	MB	MG		

Toilets:	No.	No.			Showers:	No.	No.		
WC	♂ 2	♀ 2	S	C	♟	♂ 3	♀ 3	H	Dh

1 hot each.

Directions: 3km from the centre of Safi, well signed on the northern edge of the town. Coming from the north turn right opposite the restaurants, about 200m before the Marrakech/Agadir roundabout, signed for 'Camping'. Site is in about 1km on the right.

GPS: N32°19.212' W009°14.302'

Campsite Amenities:	Local Amenities Nearby (5km or less):
Cold water sinks. Swimming pool summer only.	All 3km in Safi. Beaches 2km.

🚐 + ♂♀ = 70Dh   **All Year**   ⛺ + ♂♀ = 70Dh

OUNARA   52   D3

Camping Des Oliviers, BP13, Centre Ounagha (Ounara), Province d'Essaouira.
Tel: 0613 954382 www.campingdesoliviers.com

Excellent small campsite presented to a very good standard, an example of what can be achieved in Morocco but seldom is. The grounds are well tended. Attractive hedges with orange and lemon trees mark the pitches, which are mainly grass. All the facilities are located in a central circular block. They were clean and well maintained. The onsite restaurant prepares meals to order.

Pitch No:	Water:		Electric:			Disposal Details (sanitation):				
30	⌁	Dh	E	Amp	20Dh	⊞	MB	MG	⊡	⊟

Toilets:	No.	No.			Showers:	No.	No.		
WC	♂8	♀8	S	C	⌂	♂8	♀8	H	Dh
Unisex.					Unisex.				

Directions: 23km from Essaouira. Located in the middle of town at the Marrakech-Essaouira and Casablanca-Agadir crossroads.

GPS: N31°32.126' W009°32.883'

Campsite Amenities:
Laundry service 20Dh/kg.
Swimming pool summer only.

Local Amenities Nearby (5km or less):
All 100m in town.

🚐+♂♀= 80Dh Reduction for longer stays.   **All Year**   ⛺+♂♀= 80Dh Reduction for longer stays.

MOROCCO   MAROC

ESSAOUIRA   **54** **D3**

Camping Sidi Magdoul, Route d'Agadir, Essaouira.
Tel: 0524 472196

A pleasant campsite located behind a large sand dune 2km south of the lively and loved by everybody seaside resort of Essaouira. The campsite has clean tidy facilities equivalent to cheaper Mediterranean sites. Half of the campsite is concrete hard standing, making it ideal for long winter visits, the other half provides shaded, sandy, pitching for small units and tents. The onsite restaurant serves reasonably priced Moroccan food.

Pitch No:	Water:		Electric:		Disposal Details (sanitation):				
50	⚥ 10Dh 10Dh per tank fill.		E Amp	15Dh	⫼	MB	MG	☝	🚌

Toilets:	No.	No.			Showers:	No.	No.		
WC	♂ 4	♀ 4	S C	♿	☔	♂ 4	♀ 4	H ❄	8Dh

Directions: Agadir road. Exit Essaouira south towards Agadir. The campsite is on left in 2km, just past the small lighthouse. Turn left by the plant and pot seller, where road is no longer divided by concrete partition. Campsite 20m behind the plant and pot seller, signed.

GPS: N31°29.495' W009°45.802'

Campsite Amenities:

Local Amenities Nearby (5km or less):

All within 2 km of Essouira. Restaurant onsite. Beaches and camel trips adj.

🚐+♂♀= 44Dh   **All Year**   ⛺+♂♀= 39Dh

ARBA-IDA-OU-GOURD 55 D3

Camping le Calme, Village Ida-ou-gourd à Essaouira, 44000 Essaouira.
Tel: 0661 530413

GB F D E I CC €

An out of the way campsite, set among Argan trees extending to quite a large and very peaceful area. Facilities are modern, clean and well maintained. Pitches are unmarked and the ground is mainly grass, sand and stones being somewhat uneven, but it is possible to get level without too much difficulty. The onsite restaurant prepares meals to order. The site shop sells bread and bottled water only, which can be delivered daily. The swimming pool is open March to October.

Pitch No:	Water:			Electric:			Disposal Details (sanitation):				
80			Dh	E	10 Amp	25Dh		MB	MG		

Toilets:	No.	No.				Showers:	No.	No.			
WC	♂ 3	♀ 3	S				♂ 4	♀ 4	H		Dh
						Unisex.					

Directions: Well signed off the N1 El Jadida-Agadir road to the east of Essaouira.

GPS: N31°26.116' W009°39.480'

Campsite Amenities:

Washing machine 50Dh.

Local Amenities Nearby (5km or less):

1km in village.

🚐+♂♀= 60Dh Reduction for longer stays.   **All Year**   ⛺+♂♀= 60Dh Reduction for longer stays.

SIDI KAOUKI   58 E3

Camping Kaouki Beach, Sidi Kaouki 44000, Essaouira.
Tel: 0655 984731

Brand new campsite opened in February 2009. Good facilities are provided and were kept clean. Generous marked pitches on gravel were set amongst Argan trees providing some shade. Probable price increase for 2010. Fresh bread is delivered on a donkey each morning, direct to your pitch.

Pitch No:	Water:			Electric:			Disposal Details (sanitation):			
50			Dh	**E**	Amp	**10Dh**		MB	MG	

Toilets:	No.	No.				Showers:	No.	No.		
WC	♂ 4	♀ 4	**S**	C			♂ 4	♀ 4	**H**	Dh

Directions: Turn off the Essaouira-Agadir road around 13km south of Essaouira, signed Sidi Kaouki. The site is on the left about 300m past the beach parking area and cafés, signed.

GPS: N31°21.178' W009°47.689'

Campsite Amenities:
Cold water sinks.

Local Amenities Nearby (5km or less):
All within 1km.

🚐+♂♀= 40Dh   **All Year**   ⛺+♂♀= 40Dh

MAROC　　　　　　　　MOROCCO

SIDI KAOUKI　　　　　　　　🌙 ♋　　[59]　E3

Centre de Loisirs VHM, B.P 337 Sidi Kaouki 44000, Essaouira.
Tel: 0524 475035　www.vhm-vacances.franceserv.com

⛺ 🚐 🚍 🚙 🚌　🚐

🚐 🚐 〰 ▦ SP ▷ 🏳 🚿 🎵　GB **F** D E I　CC €

Parking on rough ground opposite the surfing beach. The shower and toilet block is new, well maintained and clean. This is an activity centre where you can go horse, camel or quad bike riding. There is an onsite restaurant and others in the village. Drinking water is provided in a plastic barrel, which is replenished daily, but is insufficient for the demand. Fresh bread is delivered on a donkey each morning, direct to your motorhome.

Pitch No:	Water:		Electric:		Disposal Details (sanitation):				
60	♿ ✗	Dh	E Amp	Dh	▥	MB	MG	🚽	▦
	Limited.								

Toilets:	No.	No.				Showers:	No.	No.		
WC	🚹 1	🚺 1	S	C	▣	🚿	🚹 1	🚺 1	H	❄ Dh

Directions: Turn off the Essaouira-Agadir road around 13km south of Essaouira, signed Sidi Kaouki. The site is on the left about 400m past the beach parking area and cafés and 100m past Camping Kaouki Beach, signed.

GPS: N31°20.878' W009°47.716'

Campsite Amenities:　　　　　　Local Amenities Nearby (5km or less):

▢ ☕ ♨ ✗ ① Wifi　　　▥ ✗ 🍴 🏠 ▥ M ▥ 🚲 〰 🔍 ⚓ 🚐 🚌
　　　　　　　　　All within 1km.

🚐+🚹🚺= 30Dh　　　**All Year**　　　⛺+🚹🚺= 20Dh

MOROCCO

MAROC

Camping Imsouane, Route de Essaouira, Imesouane, Agadir.
Tel: 0641 113413 www.morocco-camping.com

GB F D E I CC €

Recently taken over by a British/Belgian couple they have made great improvements to this once semi-derelict campsite. The land has been terraced and a new shower/toilet block constructed. The upper part of the site has marked bays but access is tight for motorhomes over 6m, the lower part is mainly unmarked. There is a fine view across the bay to the village, which is expanding from the old fishermen's dwellings built into the cliffs. The small port is relatively modern, having been constructed a few years ago. This is a popular surfing spot with the reputation of being one of the best on the Moroccan coast.

Pitch No:	Water:		Electric:			Disposal Details (sanitation):				
80	৬ ✗ Dh		E Amp	20Dh		▥	MB	MG	⏏	▦
	Drinking ask guardian.									

Toilets:	No.	No.				Showers: No.	No.			
WC	♂ 6	♀ 6	S	C	♿	♠ ♂ 6	♀ 6	H	❄	Dh

Directions: Turn off the Agadir-Essaouira road about 28km north of Tamri, where signed for the campsite. Follow the road to the village (about 8km), turn right at the 'Camping' sign and then turn right at the bottom of the hill. Look for Auberge Tasra on the right and take the track on the left just past it. Site is about 500m up the rough track.

GPS: N30°50.942' W009°49.320'

Campsite Amenities:	Local Amenities Nearby (5km or less):
◎ ⛽ 🚿 ✗ ⓘ WiFi	▼ ✗ 🛒 🏛 🚋 M 🏭 ⊘ ≈ Q ⚓ 🚌
Washing machine 30Dh	All in village 1 km. Beaches adjacent.

🚐+♂♀= 50Dh   **All Year**   ⛺+♂♀= 50Dh

IMI OUADDA   66   E3

Camping Atlantica Parc, Route d'Essaouira, Imi Ouadda, Aghroud.
Tel: 0528 820805 www.atlanticaparc.com

GB F D   CC €

Large European style campsite with comprehensive facilities including: shops, laundry, hairdresser, vehicle washing, heated pool. A gas bottle refilling service is offered and visa extensions can be arranged. This is a very busy campsite and is often full during the winter. Generally the site and facilities were clean and well maintained but may suffer overuse during busy periods. Additional space is available on the other side of the main road, beside the beach, with limited facilities, at an additional charge of 20Dh. There is a motorhome accessory shop and service/repair centre opposite the campsite entrance.

Pitch No:	Water:		Electric:	Disposal Details (sanitation):				
790		Dh	E 8 Amp 15Dh 10 Amp 20Dh 16 Amp 25Dh	IIII	MB	MG		

Toilets:	No.	No.				Showers:	No.	No.		
WC	13	13	S	C			15	15	H	Dh

Directions: On the N1 north of Agadir, 7km south of Taghazout, well signed.

GPS: N30°35.275' W009°45.056'

Campsite Amenities:	Local Amenities Nearby (5km or less):
Washing machine 35Dh. Internet 10Dh/hr.	All adjacent.

+ = 80Dh   **All Year**   + = 80Dh

MOROCCO   MAROC

Camping International, Boulevard Mohammed 5, Agadir.
Tel: 0666 185468

This is a busy urban campsite that occupies three hectares. Sadly we were refused entry so were unable to carry out an inspection and take photographs. The site information was obtained from a brief discussion with the receptionist.

Pitch No:	Water:		Electric:		Disposal Details (sanitation):
200		Dh	**E** Amp Dh		

Toilets:	No.	No.		Showers:	No.	No.
WC	👤	👤		🚿	👤	👤	Dh

Directions: On entering Agadir from the north carry straight on past the port and the turning to Marrakech, the site is on the left, signed.

GPS: N30°25.470' W009°36.480'

Campsite Amenities:

Local Amenities Nearby (5km or less):

All 1km.

🚐 +👤👤= 108Dh   **All Year**   ⛺+👤👤= Unknown

AGADIR 🕭 **72** **E3**

Paradis Nomade, Douar Azrarag, Drarga, 80000 Agadir.
Tel: 0671 121535 www.paradisnomade.com and www.paradis-nomade.com

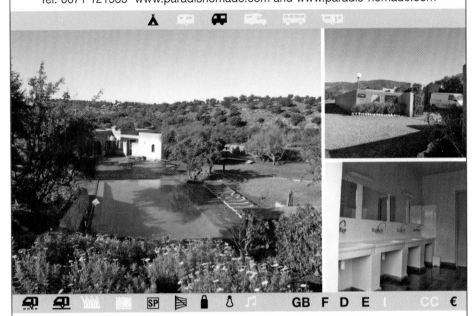

GB F D E   CC €

Very attractive and well looked after campsite that caters mainly for 4x4s. Level parking for small motorhomes or 4x4s is provided on five partly marked pitches under Argan trees. Facilities are excellent. Hot water to the showers and sinks is included in the tariff. Accommodation is offered in nomad tents on terraces and rooms are also available. Licensed bar and restaurant onsite. Accompanied 4x4, motorcycle and quad tours are available. Phone in advance to check availability of pitches.

Pitch No:	Water:	No.		Electric:			Disposal Details (sanitation):		
6	🛁	✕ Dh		E	Amp	20Dh	⨅, MS MG	🚽 In toilet.	

Toilets:	No.	No.			Showers: No.	No.		
WC 🚹 10	🚺 10	S	C ♿		🚿 🚹 10	🚺 10	H ❄	Dh
Unisex.					Unisex.			

Directions: If coming from the south or east take the Agadir eastern bypass and then turn off towards Marrakech next to the Metro hypermarket. Turn left almost immediately, opposite the entrance to Metro, and follow the 'Paradis Nomade' signs. The campsite is in about 10km. If coming from Marrakech pass through the village of Ameskroud (about 24km before Agadir) then in about 4km turn right, signed 'Agadir par Azrarg' and follow the 'Paradis Nomade' signs.
GPS: N30°28.533' W009°27.945'

Campsite Amenities: Local Amenities Nearby (5km or less):
🔲 ⛱ 🚿 ⚡ ✕ ⓘ WiFi   🍴 ✕ 🛒 🏧 🏛 M 🌆 🔗 ≈ 🔍 ⛵ 🚗 🚌
Sinks with hot water.

🚐+🚹🚺= 80Dh   **All Year**   ⛺+🚹🚺= 70Dh

SIDI OUASSAI   ⟍⟍☐ | 73 | E3

Camping International Wassay Beach, Plage Sidi Wassay, Chtouka, Aït Baha, Agadir.
Tel: 0528 217559 www.wassaybeach.com

GB F D E I   CC €

Right on the beach and adjacent to the Sous Massa National Park, this well laid out campsite opened in the autumn 2008. The site has marked gravel pitches but levelling blocks are necessary on most. The modern facilities were clean and well looked after. Access to the motorhome waste dump is difficult with a large motorhome. The tariff reduces by 10Dh per day after the 3rd day and by a further 10Dh per day after a month.

Pitch No: 78	Water: 🚰 ✗ Dh	Electric: E Amp Dh	Disposal Details (sanitation): IIII, MB MG ⊞

Toilets: No. No. WC ♂6 ♀6 S C ♿	Showers: No. No. 🚿 ♂6 ♀6 H ❄ Dh

Directions: South of Agadir turn off the N1 in Had Belfo (signed) and follow signs for about 10km. Note: some narrow village streets need to be negotiated and very large motorhomes may have difficulty.

GPS: N30°03.370' W009°41.252'

Campsite Amenities: ⊡ ☕ ⛲ ✍ ✗ (i) WiFi Cold water sinks. Washing machine 35Dh.	Local Amenities Nearby (5km or less): 🍴 ✗ 🏠 🏛 M 🏰 ≋ 🎣 🏖 🚐 Restaurant in village 500m. Tourist attraction, Sous Massa National Park. Beach adjacent.

🚐+♂♀= 70Dh   **All Year**   ⛺+♂♀= 70Dh

Riad Assllaf, Route de Tafraout, Tiznit.
Tel: 0528 600385

This is a brand new campsite that opened in 2009. It is located at an events centre specialising in weddings, conferences and parties. The motorhome parking is currently situated in the courtyard in front of the main building, but expansion is planned to the side and rear. Currently the shower and toilets are located within the main building, but a dedicated facility for the camping area is in progress and will be completed in time for winter 2009/10. Judging by the existing facilities, they are likely to be of a high standard. Also planned is a restaurant service and WiFi internet access.

Pitch No:	Water:		Electric:		Disposal Details (sanitation):				
30 More planned.			**E** 6 Amp 20 Amp	**18Dh** **25Dh**		MB	MG		

Toilets:	No.	No.			Showers:	No.	No.		
WC	♂ 11	♀ 11	**S**	**C**		♂ 1	♀ 1	**H**	**10Dh**

Directions: Heading out of Tiznit on the Tafraout road, the site is on the right at the edge of the town.

GPS: N29°41.791' W009°42.638'

Campsite Amenities:	Local Amenities Nearby (5km or less):
Laundry service available.	All 1km in Tiznit.

+♂♀= 66Dh | **All Year** | **+♂♀= 54Dh**

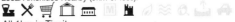

Camping International, Tiznit.
Tel: 0528 601354

Right next to the city walls, this is a very busy campsite. Most pitches were occupied with over-wintering French campers. There was a large unofficial overnight parking area on waste ground opposite the campsite but this had been cleared of motorhomes when we returned for a second visit, it was unclear whether this was a permanent arrangement. The campsite feels overcrowded and the facilities are neither very clean nor well maintained.

Pitch No:	Water:	Electric:	Disposal Details (sanitation):
240	Dh	E Amp 11Dh	MB MG

Toilets:	No.	No.	Showers:	No.	No.
WC	♁8	♁8 S C		♁6	♁6 H 7Dh
Unisex.			Unisex.		

Directions: Coming from Agadir on the N1 turn right at the first roundabout, signed. The campsite is in on the right in 200m.

GPS: N29°41.621' W009°43.561'

Campsite Amenities:
Cold water sinks.

Local Amenities Nearby (5km or less):
All within 500m.

🚐+♁♁= 48Dh   **All Year**   ⛺+♁♁= 38Dh

Camping Aglou Plage, Aglou Plage, Tiznit
Tel: 0528 613234

     GB F D E CC €

A large exposed campsite with a view over the village and the beach 500m away. The site had recently doubled in size. The newer part is slightly sloping and had no electric points in February 2009. The original site is part terraced with hard gravel and sand surface, but has no marked pitches. A new facilities block was under construction. This is urgently required as the sanitation facilities were no longer adequate and were suffering from overuse but worse still insufficient cleaning. Free WiFi is available close to the reception.

Pitch No:	Water:		Electric:		Disposal Details (sanitation):			
250	🚰	Dh	**E** 6 Amp 15Dh 16 Amp 25Dh		IIIII,	MG	🔲	

Toilets:	No.	No.		Showers:	No.	No.		
WC	🚹 2	🚺 2	S	🚿	🚹 2	🚺 2	H	Dh

Directions: Coming from Tiznit, the campsite is on the right on the edge of the town. Coming from Sidi Ifni, turn left and the site is in about 100m on the right.

GPS: N29°48.217' W009°49.640'

Campsite Amenities:	Local Amenities Nearby (5km or less):
🔲 🛒 📶 ✖ WiFi	🔲 ✖ ≋ 🏧 🚌
Cold water sinks. WiFi 50m from reception.	All within 500m.

🚐+🚹🚺= 60Dh   **All Year**   ⛺+🚹🚺= 45Dh

Camping le Nomade, No 13, Quartier Aftas 85000, Mirleft.
Tel: 0542 723232 www.nomadetrip.com

A very small walled campsite located in a quiet part of the town, about 400m from the beach. The facilities were clean when inspected. It may be possible to empty waste tanks down a manhole in the road just outside the site. All services are available in the main part of town, including quad hire.

Pitch No:	Water:			Electric:			Disposal Details (sanitation):				
7	🚰	✗ Dh		**E**	Amp	**10Dh**	▥	MB	MG	🚽	
										In toilet.	

Toilets:	No.	No.				Showers:	No.	No.		
WC	🚹 1	🚺 1	**S**	C	♿	🚿	🚹 1	🚺 1	**H**	❄ Dh

Directions: Coming from Tiznit in the town centre turn right at the crossroads, signed. After about 200m bear left to pass between the new school and the houses, then turn right between the houses, signed. Site is on the right in around 800m.

GPS: N29°34.793' W010°02.610'

Campsite Amenities:	Local Amenities Nearby (5km or less):
🔟 💤 🛗 ✗ ⓘ WiFi	🎣 ✗ 🛒 🏛 ▦ M 🔥 ≈ 🔍 🏖 ⛴ 🚌
Washing machine 30Dh.	All in 1km at Mirleft.

🚐+🚹🚺= 60Dh	**All Year**	Å+🚹🚺= 60Dh

SIDI IFNI — 82 — F3

Camping El Barco, Plage Sidi Ifni, Sidi Ifni.
Tel: 0528 780707 www.elbarco-ifni.com

SP GB F D E I NL CC €

This is a popular campsite idyllically located right on the beach below the cliffs, but can be exposed in bad weather. The pitches on hard sand and gravel are marked but not separated. The facilities are clean and well maintained. Free WiFi has a good signal up to about 60m from the reception also tables with plug sockets are provided. There are bars and restaurants nearby. The town is a short walk uphill. Everything you may desire is there including a daily fresh fish and vegetable market. Sidi Ifni has a popular surfing beach.

Pitch No:	Water:	Electric:	Disposal Details (sanitation):
100	Dh	E Amp 15Dh	MB MG

Toilets:	No.	No.			Showers:	No.	No.		
WC	4	4	S	C		4	4	H	Dh

Directions: On entering the town from the north go through the new part of town, down the hill and cross the oued, then take the first road on the right, signed for 'Hotel Aït Baamrane'. Turn left at the end of the road and the site is straight ahead.

GPS: N29°22.953' W010°10.575'

Campsite Amenities: WiFi
Washing service 10Dh/kg.

Local Amenities Nearby (5km or less): M
Market (souk) Sunday. All in town 500m.

+ = 60Dh **All Year** **+ = 50Dh**

Camping Sidi Ifni
Tel: 0528 876734

GB F D E   CC €

Next to the beach this is a popular campsite. A high wall provides shelter from the wind, unfortunately it also blocks the sea view but a gate gives direct access to the beach. Unmarked pitches are on hard sand and gravel. The facilities are old but clean. Free WiFi service. The site is conveniently located with a bar and restaurants nearby and it is only a short walk uphill to the town. The town has everything you need including a daily fresh fish and vegetable market. Sidi Ifni has a popular surfing beach.

Pitch No:	Water:			Electric:			Disposal Details (sanitation):			
80		Dh		E	Amp	Dh		MB	MG	

Toilets:	No.	No.				Showers:	No.	No.		
WC	♂ 4	♀ 4	S	C			♂ 2	♀ 2	H	Dh

Directions: On entering the town from the north go through the new part of town, down the hill and across the oued, and then take the first road on the right, signed for 'Hotel Aït Baamrane'. Site is on the right in 100m, signed.

GPS: N29°23.042' W010°10.390'

Campsite Amenities:
WiFi
Cold water sinks. Swimming pool summer only.

Local Amenities Nearby (5km or less):
M
Market (souk) Sunday. All in town 500m.

🚐+♂♀= 60Dh   **All Year**   ⛺+♂♀= 30Dh

SIDI IFNI 84 F3

Camping Municipal, Sidi Ifni.

GB F

This basic campsite is popular with long stay visitors because of the low tariff and being conveniently close to the shops in the older part of the town. The site is walled so there is no sea view, also it is a long steep walk to the beach. Pitches are in rows on hard sand and gravel with each row divided by a border of small trees and shrubs. Facilities are old but fairly clean. A short level walk takes you to all services including a daily fresh fish and vegetable market, restaurants and banks. Nearby building work caused some daytime noise at the time of inspection. It is possible that the site may be enlarged for 2010.

Pitch No:	Water:	Electric:	Disposal Details (sanitation):
67	5Dh	E 20Dh	

Toilets:	No.	No.			Showers:	No.	No.
WC	3	3	S	C		2	2

Directions: On entering the town from the north go through the new part of town, down the hill and across the oued, then straight on up the hill. At the top turn right at the T-junction then bear left. Turn left at the roundabout in front of the hospital. Take the second road on the right (opposite the Pharmacia El Ouafi) and the site entrance is in front of you.

GPS: N29°22.713' W010°10.810'

Campsite Amenities:

Cold sinks & laundry service possible.

Local Amenities Nearby (5km or less):

Market (souk) Sunday. All in town 500m.

+ = 32Dh **All Year** **+ = 28Dh**

GUELMIM   🔔 | 85 | F3

Fort Bou Jerif, BP504, 81000, Guelmim.
Tel: 0672 130017 www.fortboujerif.com

🏕 🚐 🚙 🚍 🚌 🚎

🔌 🔌 ♨ 🏞 SP 🏞 🍾 △ 🎵   **GB** **F** D E I   CC €

Anyone expecting to find the campsite at an old fort will be disappointed, the remains of the original fort are about 1km further on down the track towards the coast but parking is possible there. The new Fort Bou Jerif is very attractive and comprises a small hotel and restaurant, with a camping area to the rear. The pitches are unmarked and there is no shade, nevertheless the site has a very peaceful feel to it and the facilities are clean and well maintained. Electricity is from the site's own generator and is only available in the evening up to 11pm. The coast is a few km past the site, along a rough track, reputedly there is good sea fishing. Advice on fishing and arrangements for walking or 4x4 trips can all be obtained from the reception. Accommodation in rooms or nomad tents is also available.

Pitch No:	Water:		Electric:			Disposal Details (sanitation):				
100	🚰	⚒ Dh	**E** Amp Dh			IIII	MB	MG	🚽	🚐
			Evenings only.						In toilet.	

Toilets:	No.	No.				Showers:	No.	No.		
WC 🚹 16	🚹 16	**S**	**C**	♿		🚿 🚹 10	🚹 10	**H**	❄	10Dh
Unisex.						Unisex.				

Directions: In Guelmim take the road towards Sidi Ifni, just as you leave the town take the left turn signed 'Plage Blanche' and 'Fort Bou Jerif'. Follow the Plage Blanche and Fort Bou Jerif signs until you see the track to Fort Bou Jerif signed on the right. Follow the track for about 9km to the site. Note that the track may be rough in places and can suffer from wind blown sand. Motorhomes with long rear overhangs or low ground clearance should probably not attempt to drive down this track.
GPS: N29°04.839' W010°19.831'

Campsite Amenities:	Local Amenities Nearby (5km or less):
🅾 ☕ 🛒 ⚡ ✗ ⓘ WiFi	🛒 ✗ 🛒 🏠 🚂 M 🏛 🌿 ≋ ⚓ 🏖 🚗 🚍
Cold water sinks. Bread ordering.	

🚐 +🚹🚹= 90Dh   **All Year**   🏕+🚹🚹= 90Dh

MAROC MOROCCO

Camping Atlantique, Boulevard Hassan II, 82000 El Ouatia.

The site is a walled bungalow complex providing some shelter from the wind. There is a large motorhome parking area. The facilities were a good standard and kept clean, though water pressure was low to non-existent at times. At the time of visit (Feb 2009) additional facilities were under construction. There is a small supermarket just outside the site.

Motorhomes park overnight in various parts of Tan Tan Plage but local authorities are discouraging this. Paying a guardian at a parking area does not guarantee that the police will not move you on!

Pitch No:	Water:		Electric:		Disposal Details (sanitation):				
50	🚰	Dh	E	Amp Dh				🚪	

Toilets: No.	No.				Showers: No.	No.		
WC 👤1	👤1	S	C		🚿 👤2	👤2	H	Dh
Unisex.					Unisex.			

Directions: On entering Tan Tan Plage carry straight on towards the port, then turn right where signed to 'Hotel de France'. Pass Camping Sable d'Or and Hotel de France in 1km and drive a further 500m.

GPS: N28°29.789' W011°20.171'

Campsite Amenities:	Local Amenities Nearby (5km or less):
📷 🐕	🍽️ 🛒 🏛️ 🔍
Washing machine 30Dh. Cold water sinks.	All 500m in town. Beach 200m.

+👤👤= 60Dh **All Year** +👤👤= 60Dh

EL OUATIA (TAN TAN PLAGE) 88 F2

Camping Sable D'Or, Bvd Hassan II, 82000 El Ouatia.
Tel: 0528 879080

GB F D E I CC €

This site is a partly walled bungalow complex with parking for motorhomes around the central block. There is a separate sanitary block for campers but at the time of our visit the showers were not working and one of the bungalows was in use for this purpose. Unmarked pitches are on hard sand and gravel, with a view to sea across waste ground. Facilities were cleaned once a day but suffered from sand ingress. Note: water pressure was low to non-existent at times.

Motorhomes park overnight in various parts of Tan Tan Plage but local authorities are discouraging this. Paying a guardian at a parking area does not guarantee that the police will not move you on!

Pitch No:	Water:			Electric:			Disposal Details (sanitation):				
30			Dh	E	Amp	Dh		MB	MG		

Toilets:	No.		No.				Showers:	No.		No.		
WC	1		1	S	C			1		1	H	Dh

Directions: On entering Tan Tan Plage carry straight on towards the port, and then turn right where signed to 'Hotel de France'. The campsite is on left in about 1km, opposite the Hotel de France.

GPS: N28°29.649' W011°20.245'

Campsite Amenities:
Laundry service.

Local Amenities Nearby (5km or less):
All 500m in town. Beach 200m.

+ = 60Dh   **All Year**   **+ = 60Dh**

EL OUATIA (TAN TAN PLAGE) 89 F2

Camping des 2 Chameaux, 82000 El Ouatia.
Tel: 0618 490681 www.aaubergecampingdes2chameaux.com

GB F D E I CC €

The campsite is in a large walled courtyard behind the Auberge and restaurant. Unmarked pitches are on hard sand. An attractive small indoor sitting area is available for clients, as is a small kitchen. Facilities are very clean and well maintained.

Motorhomes park overnight in various parts of Tan Tan Plage but local authorities are discouraging this. Paying a guardian at a parking area does not guarantee that the police will not move you on!

Pitch No:	Water:			Electric:			Disposal Details (sanitation):				
50	🚰	✕	Dh	E	Amp	15Dh	▥	ME	MG	🔳	🚐

Toilets:	No.	No.				Showers:	No.	No.			
WC ♂♀ 5	♂♀ 5	S	C	♿		🚿 ♂♀ 4	♂♀ 4	H	❄	Dh	
Unisex.						Unisex.					

Directions: At the turning to Laayoune, just before Tan Tan Plage.

GPS: N28°29.264' W011°19.321'

Campsite Amenities:	Local Amenities Nearby (5km or less):
🗄 🧺 ♨ ✂ ✕ ⓘ WiFi	⚡ ✕ 🛒 🏛 ▦ M ⛽ ∅ ≈ 🔍 ⚓ 🛥 🚌 🚐
Washing machine 40Dh. Cold water sinks.	All about 2km in town.

🚐+♂♀= 95Dh   **All Year**   △+♂♀= 95Dh

MOROCCO

MAROC

Camping Le Roi Bedouin, BP830 Laayoune 7000.
Tel: 0667 925874 www.geocities.com/le_roi_bedouin

⛺ 🚐 🚍 🚐 🚌 🚐

🔌 🚿 ♨ 🔲 SP 📋 🔥 ♪ **GB F D** E I CC €

This is a unique, small and peaceful semi-desert campsite that after rain is alongside a small river and waterfall. There is a superb view out to the Oum Dba salt lake. The Belgian campsite owners can advise on walking and 4x4 routes in the area. Water comes from the site's own well but the salty taste makes it undrinkable. Facilities are well maintained and clean. Water is solar heated for the showers. Tented accommodation is available and meals are made to order.

Pitch No:	Water:			Electric:			Disposal Details (sanitation):				
12	🚰	⊠	Dh	E	Amp	Dh	🚽,	MB	MG	🚪	🚐

Toilets:	No.	No.					Showers:	No.	No.		
WC	♂2	♂2	S	C	♿		🚿 ♂3	♂3	H	❄	Dh
Unisex.							Unisex.				

Directions: On the N1 south of Daoura village, about 35km north of Laayoune. Turn onto the piste at the sign for the campsite. The site is in 4.5km down a passable track but care must be taken! Owners of motorhomes with low ground clearance or long rear overhangs should inspect the road prior to driving it. After rain, which is rare, access may be limited to four-wheel drive vehicles only.
GPS: N27°27.848' W013°03.104'

Campsite Amenities:
📻 🍽 ⚒ ⚱ ✖ ⓘ WiFi
Cold water sinks. Restaurant to order.

Local Amenities Nearby (5km or less):
🍴 ✖ 🛒 🏠 🎰 M 🐾 ⚱ ≈ 🏖 ⚓ 🚂

Camping Nil.

A large, bare, sandy campsite, walled to give some shelter from the wind. Facilities are old and not well maintained, but were fairly clean. Most of the electric points were not working. Motorhomes not staying at the site can refill water and empty toilets for 30Dh.

Pitch No:	Water:	Electric:	Disposal Details (sanitation):
100 (30 with electric points).	💧 Dh	**E** Amp **10Dh**	🚽 In toilet.

Toilets:	No.	No.		Showers:	No.	No.		
WC	♂ 12	♀ 12	S **C**	🚿	♂ 12	♀ 12	H ❄	Dh
Unisex.				Unisex.				

Directions: In Laayoune follow signs to the airport, the road continues on to Foum el Oued, passing a Samir supermarket on the way. The site is signed on the left just before the town and is 100m down a sandy track.

GPS: N27°10.732' W013°23.616'

Campsite Amenities:	Local Amenities Nearby (5km or less):
Cold water sinks.	200m in town.

🚐+♂♀= 40Dh   **All Year**   🏕+♂♀= 40Dh

MOROCCO

MAROC

Camping International Porte du Sahara, Route Agadir, C.R. Abaynou, 81000 Guelmim.

This campsite was only part finished and the completion date is unknown. Pitches are marked by rows of small trees and most look to have insufficient space for motorhomes. There are no showers; no electricity and the two toilets were dirty. There seems to be a general lack of interest in appealing to European clients.

Pitch No:	Water:			Electric:			Disposal Details (sanitation):				
100		Dh		E	Amp	Dh		MB	MG	🚽 In toilet	

Toilets:	No.	No.				Showers:	No.	No.			
WC	♂ 1	♀ 1	S	C					H		Dh

Directions: On the N1 from Guelmim to Agadir, about 3km from Guelmim.

GPS: N29°01.182' W010°01.656'

Campsite Amenities:
Cold water sinks.

Local Amenities Nearby (5km or less):
All 3km in Guelmim.

 🚐+♂♀= 60Dh   All Year   ⛺+♂♀= 60Dh

ABAYNOU   98   F3

Camping de la Station Thermale, Abaynou, Guelmim.

Three camping areas support the thermal baths. The first (Camping No 1) is the original small walled campsite. The others are in the parking areas for the thermal baths, one by the women's baths and one by the men's baths. The location is popular and the sites are likely to be busy. Facilities are basic and not particularly clean. After 7pm mixed use of the baths by Europeans is permitted, the women's baths is reportedly in a better state than the men's. If these sites are full, Camping Britta Dancy is about 2km beyond Abaynou, along a rough track. The restaurant is at campsite 3.

Pitch No:	Water:			Electric:			Disposal Details (sanitation):				
40	🚰	✗	Dh	E	Amp	20Dh		MB	MC	🔳	

Toilets:	No.	No.				Showers:	No.	No.			
WC	♂3	♀3	S	C	♿	🚿	♂3	♀3	H	❄	Dh
Unisex.						Unisex.					

Directions: Abaynou is signed to the right, heading out of Guelmim towards Sidi Ifni. There are three sites within the village, all associated with the thermal baths.

GPS: N29°05.759' W010°01.123'

Campsite Amenities:	Local Amenities Nearby (5km or less):
📷 🛒 ♨ ⚓ ✗ ① WiFi	💺 ✗ 🛒 🏪 🚋 M 🏰 ✏ ≋ ⛱ 🛖 🚌
Cold water sinks.	All in village.

🚐+♂♀= 40Dh   **All Year**   ⛺+♂♀= N/A

OASIS DE TIGHMERT

99 F3

Hotel Facom Tour, Oasis de Tighmert, Guelmim.

GB F

At the time of our visit the site was closed for 'works', the guardian told us that it would re-open in a few months 'Inshallah'.

Pitch No: Water: Electric: Disposal Details (sanitation):

Dh   Amp   Dh

Toilets: No.   No.   Showers: No.   No.

S C   H   Dh

Directions: Take the N12 east from Guelmin towards Fask & Assa, after about 3km turn right, signed Asrir. Go through Asrir towards Tighmert. At Tighmert the site is signed on the right just before you reach the radio masts.

GPS: N28°56.933' W009°57.347'

Campsite Amenities: Local Amenities Nearby (5km or less):

+ = Unknown   All Year   + = Unknown

OASIS DE TIGHMERT `100` F3

Camping Coeur de l'Oasis, Oasis de Tighmert, Guelmim.
Tel: 0678 396342

GB F D E I S

Visitors are welcomed as part of the family, to this small, friendly, family run campsite that opened in 2008 and is slowly being developed. At the time of inspection the facilities comprised of a single shower and toilet that was shared with the family. Electricity was supplied from a socket in the house, but plans are in hand for improvements. Traditional home cooked Moroccan meals are available to order.

Pitch No:	Water:	Electric:	Disposal Details (sanitation):
30	Dh	E Amp 15Dh	

Toilets:	No.	No.	Showers:	No.	No.
WC	♀1	♂1 S	♀1	♂1 H	Dh
Unisex.			Unisex.		

Directions: Take the N12 east from Guelmin towards Fask & Assa, after about 3km turn right, signed Asrir. Go through Asrir towards Tighmert. At Tighmert go past the radio masts and the school on your right then take the track to the right (unsigned) the site is in a few hundred metres, behind the red metal gates.

GPS: N28°56.804' W009°56.759'

Campsite Amenities:

Local Amenities Nearby (5km or less):
Shop in village. Tourist attraction - palmerai.

🚐+♀♂= 35Dh   **All Year**   ⛺+♀♂= 25Dh

GUELMIM   **101**   **F3**

Domaine Khattab, Route d'Assa Zag, Guelmim.
Tel: 0661 176411

Part shaded | GB F D E I | CC €

Located on a 22ha farm this is a family run campsite. About 40 of the pitches are individually marked with small trees. The remainder are larger and can be used for longer stays or by groups of friends travelling together. Facilities are slightly rustic but are kept clean. Electricity is generated by a rather noisy generator and is only available for about 3 hours in the evening. Water is drawn from the site's own well, but we were assured that it was treated and potable. Traditional Moroccan meals are available to order. The owner's son is a mechanic; he can make small repairs on site as well as carry out solar panel installations. Desert tours by 4x4 or camel can be arranged.

Pitch No:	Water:	Electric:	Disposal Details (sanitation):				
51	Dh Drinking ask guardian.	**E** Amp **10Dh** 3hrs.		MB	MG		

Toilets:	No.	No.		Showers:	No.	No.		
WC	♂ 4	♀ 4	S C	♒	♂ 3	♀ 3	H	10Dh

Directions: N12. About 12km east from Guelmin towards Fask & Assa. The campsite is signed off the N12 on the right, take the track for about 800m.

GPS: N28°58.203' W009°57.004'

Campsite Amenities: Local Amenities Nearby (5km or less):

Washing service price negotiable.

🚐 + ♂♀ = 40Dh   **All Year**   ⛺ + ♂♀ = 40Dh

MAROC

MOROCCO

Camping Tazka, Tafraout.
Tel: 0528 801428 www.campingtazka.com

GB F · D E I · CC €

Opened in 2005 this walled campsite is in the palmerai but outside of the town. There are no marked pitches but some shade is available. Facilities are good, clean and well maintained. Meals are available to order.

Pitch No:	Water:		Electric:			Disposal Details (sanitation):				
40	⚡	Dh	**E**	Amp	**20Dh**	▥	MB	**MG**	🗗	

Toilets:	No.	No.			Showers:	No.	No.			
WC	♂ 3	♀ 3	**S**	C	♿	♁ ♂ 3	♀ 3	**H**	❄	**10Dh**

Directions: Coming from Tiznit, site is on right (signposted) 2 km before Tafraout.

GPS: N29°43.088' W008°59.218'

Campsite Amenities:
▣ ☕ ⛲ ≤ ✗ ⓘ WiFi
Cold water sinks.

Local Amenities Nearby (5km or less):
⚡ ✗ ... 🚌
All 2km in town.

Camping les Trois Palmiers, Tafraout.
Tel: 0662 425870

GB F D E I CC €

This walled campsite is located close to the town. Within the campsite walls there is room for 25 motorhomes. On land controlled by the campsite outside the walls there is space for another 80 vehicles. Occupants parked outside the walls have access to the campsite facilities but only vehicles closest to the wall may be able to hook up to electricity. The pitch fees are the same for inside or outside. Facilities are old but appeared relatively clean.

Pitch No:	Water:			Electric:			Disposal Details (sanitation):				
105		Dh		E	Amp	17.5Dh		MB	MG		

Toilets:	No.	No.				Showers:	No.	No.			
WC	3	3	S	C			2	2	H		10Dh
Unisex.						Unisex.					

Directions: On the R104 coming from Tiznit bear left on entering the town and the site is on the left in a few hundred metres.

GPS: N29°43.453' W008°58.789'

Campsite Amenities: Local Amenities Nearby (5km or less):

Cold water sinks.   All 500m in town.

+ = 35Dh   **All Year**   + = 35Dh

MAROC

MOROCCO

EL GUERDANE · 105 · E4

Le Jardin de la Koudya, BP391 El Guerdane, Taroudant.
Tel: 0665 798722 http://koudya.com

GB F D E I CC €

This is an unusual campsite located on a farm that supplies organic produce to British supermarkets. The French owner is keen to develop a small, quality site and in March 2009 there were just 6 pitches with limited shower and toilet facilities. On a separate part of the farm a further 16 pitches with additional toilets and showers are planned to be available for the 2009/10 winter season. Campers are free to walk around the farm and also have the use of an attractive private garden and small swimming pool. An onsite shop sells mainly organic produce and meals can be prepared to order. Visits and tours can be organised.

Pitch No:	Water:	Electric:		Disposal Details (sanitation):
22	丞	E	22Dh	▥, 🖪

Toilets: No. No.			Showers: No. No.		
🚻 †1 †1 S			☌ †1 †1 H	10Dh
Unisex.			Unisex.	

Directions: On the N10 Agadir to Taroudant road around 14km from Taroudant.

GPS: N30°25.128' W009°02.438'

Campsite Amenities:
Washing machine 33Dh.

Local Amenities Nearby (5km or less):
Small shop across the road.

🚐+†† = 55Dh   All Year   Å+†† = N/A

TALIOUINE   107   E4

Camping Toubkal, BP98 Taliouine.
Tel: 0528 534343 www.maghrebtourism.com/aubergetoubkal

GB F D E I CC €

A well-kept and attractive campsite with several terraced camping areas, all with views across the valley. Sanitary facilities are in three well-maintained and clean blocks; water is solar heated for showers. A visit to the swimming pool costs 20Dh and WiFi is planned. This is a good base to visit the safron-producing area around Taliouine. You can also visit the Souktana co-operative, for more information visit http://www.oasisdemezgarne.com/lgen/Boutique/saffron-shop.htm
On Mondays there is a souk at the Kasbah.

Pitch No:	Water:			Electric:			Disposal Details (sanitation):				
60		Dh		E	Amp	20Dh		MB	MG		

Toilets:	No.	No.				Showers:	No.	No.			
WC	♂7	♀7	S	C	♿	♿	♂3	♀3	H	❄	Dh
Unisex.						Unisex.					

Directions: N10. From Ouarzazate the campsite is located about 1.5km before Taliouine.

GPS: N30°31.362' W007°53.629'

Campsite Amenities:	Local Amenities Nearby (5km or less):
Washing machine 30Dh.	All 1.5km in town.

🚐 + ♂♀ = 40Dh   **All Year**   ⛺ + ♂♀ = 40Dh

MARRAKECH
109 D4

Camping-Car Maroc, BP 4100 Amerchich, Marrakech Amerchich 40002.
Tel: 0661 95 55 17 www.campingcarmaroc.com

GB F D E I   CC €

This is a newly developed campsite and many of the facilities were still under construction at the time of our visit in March 2009. The French owners are dedicated to producing an exceptionally high quality site and intend by the end of 2009 to have completed construction of a large pool, restaurant, bar, Jacuzzi and hammam. There will be a price increase for winter 2009/10. Pitches are well laid out, gravelled and fully serviced with water and electric points. Newly planted trees & shrubs provide privacy and some shade, There is a well-stocked motorhome accessory shop and motorhomes are available for hire. The site offers a range of options to visit Marrakech, from a free lift to the nearest bus stop to a personal tour service. 4x4 and camel trips can also be arranged.

Pitch No:	Water:			Electric:		Disposal Details (sanitation):				
25			Dh	E	30Dh	▥	MB	MG	▯	🚌
				Euro sockets.						

Toilets:	No.	No.				Showers:	No.	No.		
WC	👤2	👤2	S	C	♿	🚿	👤2	👤2	H	❄ Dh

Directions: N9 Marrakech to Ouarzazate. Turn off the N9 at the campsite signs about 12km from Marrakech. The site is approx 2.5km down the unmade track. Well signed.

GPS: N31°36.822' W007°53.421'

Campsite Amenities:
Washing service 80Dh.
Internet 20Dh/hr, 100Dh/day.

Local Amenities Nearby (5km or less):
2.5km to bus stop. Camping shop onsite.

🚐 + 👤👤 = 80Dh Price increase expected   **All Year**   ⛺ + 👤👤 = None

Camping Ferdaous, Route de Casablanca, Marrakech.
Tel: 0524 304090

⛺ 🚐 🚙 🚐 🚌 🚃

🚐 🚐 〰️ ▦ SP ⚑ 🔒 ♨️ 🎵   GB F D E I   CC €

Located alongside the main Casablanca road this large flat campsite is part shaded by trees but has no marked pitches. There is a new sanitary block and a rather dilapidated old block that remains in use. Resident peacocks, true to form, can be noisy. There is a regular minibus service from the campsite into Marrakech: one to four people costs 40Dh then 10Dh per additional person. Tours of the city can be arranged, ask the driver.

Pitch No:	Water:		Electric:		Disposal Details (sanitation):			
140	🚰	✖ Dh	**E**	Amp **25Dh**	IIII,	MB	**MG**	🏚 🚽

Toilets:	No.	No.			Showers:	No.	No.		
WC	♂ 18	♀ 18	**S**	**C** ♿	🚿	♂ 12	♀ 12	**H**	❄ Dh

Directions: On the N9 Casablanca road about 11km from Marrakech, alongside the CHM fuel station.

GPS: N31°43.322' W007°58.963'

Campsite Amenities:	Local Amenities Nearby (5km or less):
🅾 🧺 ⚒ ⚔ ✖ ⓘ WiFi	🔋 ✖ 🛒 🏛 🚂 M 〽 🎣 ≋ 🔍 ⛰ 🚗 🚌
Cold water sinks.	Supermarket 4km.

🚐+♂♀= 46Dh   **All Year**   ⛺+♂♀= 42Dh

MARRAKECH　　　　　　　　　　　　　　　🏭　**111**　**D4**

Le Relais de Marrakech.
Tel: 0664 717328 www.lerelaisdemarrakech.com

This is the nearest campsite to the city and around 5 minutes drive from the Marjane hypermarket. It is a pleasant open site with attractive grounds around the swimming pool and 'Kasbah'. Pitches are marked though there is no physical separation but a tree-planting programme is under way. Free WiFi service is provided on buying a drink at the bar. Bottled water and bread is available to order. A taxi booking service is available, a taxi to Marrakech costs 60Dh.

Pitch No:	Water:		Electric:			Disposal Details (sanitation):				
140		Dh	E	Amp	25Dh	⬛.	MB	MG	🚽	🚌

Toilets:	No.	No.				Showers:	No.	No.		
WC	🚹3	🚺3	S	C		🚿	🚹3	🚺3	H	Dh
Unisex.						Unisex.				

Directions: From the north take the N9 towards Marrakech, about 5km after the motorway junction turn right, sp Safi then follow signs to Sangho and the small campsite signs. From Marrakech follow the signs to Casablanca, then Safi, then as above.

GPS: N31°42.619' W007°59.324'

Campsite Amenities:	Local Amenities Nearby (5km or less):
🔘 ☕ ⚒ ⚲ ✗ ⓘ WiFi	🧺 ✗ 🛒
Washing service 60Dh.	Supermarket 3km.

🚐+🚹🚺= 70Dh　　　**All Year**　　　⛺+🚹🚺= 70Dh

TAMDAKHT 112   E5

Auberge Camping Defat Kasbah, Douar Assfalou, Tamdakht, 45000 Äit Benhaddou, Ouarzazate. Tel: 0524 888020 www.defatkasbah.com

GB F D E I   CC €

Parking area at the rear of the Auberge. There is a flat, hard gravel area with no shade but there is a view across the valley. Facilities were ok but not particularly clean.

Pitch No:	Water:		Electric:		Disposal Details (sanitation):			
20	Dh	E	Amp	10Dh		MB	MG	In toilet.

Toilets:	No.	No.			Showers:	No.	No.		
WC	3	3	S	C		2	2	H	10Dh
Unisex.					Unisex.				

Directions: From Aït Benhaddou drive 5km towards Telouet. Auberge Camping is on the right immediately before the river bridge. The campsite is through an archway (max dimensions 4m high x 3.5m wide).

GPS: N31°04.277' W007°08.500'

Campsite Amenities:	Local Amenities Nearby (5km or less):
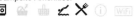 WiFi	
Washing service 10Dh/kg. Swimming pool summer only.	All 5km Aït Benhaddou.

+ = 60Dh   **All Year**   + = 50Dh

AÏT BENHADDOU  **113** **E5**

Auberge Camping Kasbah du Jardin, Aït Benhaddou, Ouarzazate.
Tel: 0524 888019 www.kasbahdujardin.com

GB F D E I   CC €

This is the closest campsite to the Kasbah, which is a few minutes walk away. Pitches are surfaced with hard sand and gravel but have no shade. Facilities were ok, but a general lack off attention to keeping things clean and tidy lets them down. This site has the advantage of a usable motorhome service area for emptying grey and black tanks.

Pitch No:	Water:			Electric:			Disposal Details (sanitation):				
20			Dh	E	Amp	30Dh	ⅢⅢ	MB	MG	⌂	🚌

Toilets:	No.	No.				Showers:	No.	No.		
WC	♂3	♀3	S	C		♂2	♀2	H		10Dh
Unisex.						Unisex.				

Directions: From the N9 drive toward the village and the site is on the right about 1km past the main parking area for the Kasbah.

GPS: N31°02.823' W007°08.119'

Campsite Amenities:

Local Amenities Nearby (5km or less):
All within 500m.

🚐+♂♀= 40Dh   **All Year**   ⛺+♂♀= 40Dh

MOROCCO

MAROC

Camping le Tissa, Taborhate, Ouarzazate.
Tel: 0525 891030

GB F D E I CC €

This walled campsite has gravel pitches that are partly marked by small olive trees. Facilities were a bit dark and rustic, but fairly clean. The small restaurant serves the usual Moroccan dishes to order. About 20km from Ouarzazate and 12km from Aït Benhaddou this site is a good alternative to the often-crowded Ouarzazate campsite. There is a surcharge of 5Dh for vehicles 8m plus.

Pitch No:	Water:		Electric:		Disposal Details (sanitation):				
60		Dh	**E**	Amp	**15Dh**		MB	MG	

Toilets:	No.	No.			Showers:	No.	No.		
WC	�me 2	♀ 2	**S**	**C**		♿ 2	♀ 2	**H**	**5Dh**

Directions: On the N9 close to the turning for Aït Benhaddou.

GPS: N30°58.506' W007°05.847'

Campsite Amenities:

Cold water sinks. WiFi 10Dh/hr.

Local Amenities Nearby (5km or less):

All 500m in village.

🚐+♟= 30Dh   **All Year**   ⛺+♟= 25Dh

OUARZAZATE   116   E5

Camping Municipal Ouarzazate, 45000 Ouarzazate.
Tel: 0524 888322

SP   GB F D E I   CC €

This walled campsite has some large trees giving some shade. This is a busy site often used by groups, and can feel a bit overcrowded. Unfortunately the facilities were not being cleaned often enough for the level of use. Drinking water is from one tap only, located by the gate. The onsite restaurant has a delivery service to your pitch. The Taourit Kasbah is well worth a visit and is only about 800m in the direction of the town centre, which is around 2km from the campsite.

Pitch No:	Water:	Electric:	Disposal Details (sanitation):
90	1 drinking water tap.	E Amp 20Dh	MG

Toilets:	No.	No.		Showers:	No.	No.		
WC	♂ 4	♀ 4	S C		♂ 6	♀ 6	H	8Dh

Directions: The site is located on the eastern side of the town off the N10 towards Skoura and is well signed. It is situated alongside the Complexe Touristique.

GPS: N30°55.386' W006°53.211'

Campsite Amenities:

Cold water sinks. Shop - basics.

Local Amenities Nearby (5km or less):

All 2km in town. Tourist attraction Taourit Kasbah 800m.

🚐+♂♀= 39Dh   **All Year**   ⛺+♂♀= 34Dh

Camping Amghar
Tel: 0671 076505

Located in a lunar looking landscape the campsite is a welcome 'oasis' of green plants. This is a very small campsite that is gradually being developed by the owner. Partially marked pitches on gravel are set amongst small olive trees. A small kitchen with a gas cooker and sink is available. The slightly rustic facilities are, with the exception of the kitchen, fairly clean.

Pitch No:	Water:			Electric:		Disposal Details (sanitation):	
5	Dh			**E 16 Amp 30Dh**			
				6 Amp 15Dh			

Toilets:	No.	No.			Showers:	No.	No.	
WC 1	1	**S** C			1	1	**H**	Dh
Unisex.					Unisex.			

Directions: On the R108 road from Tazenakht - Agdz, just on the Agdz side of the village, signed.

GPS: N30°33.897' W006°45.118'

Campsite Amenities:

Washing machine 20Dh. Restaurant, food to order.

Local Amenities Nearby (5km or less):

Shop and restaurant 1km in Tasla. Public transport outside campsite.

   **= 30Dh**   **All Year**    **= 20Dh**

Camping Auberge Oasis Palmier, Amezrou, Zagora.
Tel: 0666 569750 www.oasispalmier.com

A popular campsite located in the palmerie. The pitches are mainly on firm sand and are separated by palms, shrubs and stones. Facilities are clean and well maintained. The onsite restaurant makes Moroccan meals to order, which can be served in a nomad tent or on the terrace. Tented accommodation is available also camel and 4x4 trips can be organised.

Pitch No:	Water:		Electric:			Disposal Details (sanitation):				
30		Dh	E	Amp	10Dh		MB	MG		

Toilets:	No.	No.				Showers:	No.	No.		
WC	2	2	S	C			2	2	H	Dh
Unisex.						Unisex.				

Directions: Located south of Zagora. From the north go through the town centre, then after crossing the bridge turn left, signed. Drive 300m and the site in on the left. Access is tight for large motorhomes.

GPS: N30°19.439' W005°49.576'

Campsite Amenities:	Local Amenities Nearby (5km or less):
Cold water sinks. Bread to order.	All 1.5km in Zagora.

+ = 30Dh   **All Year**   + = 30Dh

Camping Kasbah de la Palmeraie, BP23, 45050 Agdz.
Tel: 0524 843640 www.casbah-caidali.net

GB F D E I   CC €

This is an interesting campsite almost at the start of the long Draa Valley palmerai and palm trees provide shade to parts of the site. Pitches are unmarked but there are several partly separated areas. Facilities are clean and well maintained. The family who own the site have occupied the nearby Kasbah for generations. They started restoring these magnificent buildings about ten years ago. Work is being carried out by parties of volunteers and is funded by income generated from the campsite. Tours, in English, are highly recommended and give a real insight into the history and restoration of the Kasbah. Half-board rooms are available within the Kasbah at 220Dh per night.

Pitch No:	Water:	Electric:		Disposal Details (sanitation):
40	♿ ✖ Dh	**E** 3 Amp **10Dh**		
		6 Amp **13Dh**		

Toilets:	No.	No.		Showers:	No.	No.		
WC ♦4	♦4	**S**	**C** ♿	🚿 ♦4	♦4	**H** ❄	Dh	
Unisex.				Unisex.				

Directions: About 3km from the centre of town. Coming from the west: turn left in the centre of town (where the main road turns right). From the east: carry straight on in the centre of town where the main road turns left, signed for campsite, carry straight on along the road, then track, the site is on the right in about 3km, signed.
GPS: N30°42.707' W006°26.798'

Campsite Amenities:	Local Amenities Nearby (5km or less):
🔲 ☕ 🏪 ♨ ✖ ⓘ WiFi	🔫 ✖ 🍴 🏬 🏛 M 🏔 🚲 ≈ 🔍 ⛽ 🚍
Laundry service. Restaurant from mid 2009. 1 computer, WiFi planned.	Shop and restaurant in Agdz around 3km. Tourist attraction onsite. Public transport in Agdz.

 **+♦♦= 46Dh**   **All Year**   **+♦♦= 36Dh**

Camping Prends ton Temps, BP167 Zagora 45900.
Tel: 0524 846543 www.prendstontemps.com

Near the centre of town this is a popular, small campsite with music most evenings. A variety of reasonably priced accommodation makes this site popular with young travellers. This site is also popular with campervan and motorhome users. Unmarked pitches under palm trees have some shade. Facilities were clean. Meals are cooked to order and can be served under the palms.

Pitch No:	Water:			Electric:			Disposal Details (sanitation):				
14	🚰	✗	Dh	**E** Inc.	Amp	Dh	IIII.	MB	MG	📵 In toilet.	

Toilets:	No.	No.			♿	Showers:	No.	No.			
WC Unisex.	🚹 3	🚺 3	S	C		🚿 Unisex.	🚹 3	🚺 3	H	❄	Dh

Directions: From the north as you drive into Zagora turn left at the yellow 'Camping Prends ton Temps' signs. Drive 600m down an unmade road (due to be surfaced 2009). Follow the signs until you see the yellow gates of the site on your right.

GPS: N30°20.265' W005°49.924'

Campsite Amenities:	Local Amenities Nearby (5km or less):
🔲 🐕 🧺 ✗ ⓘ WiFi	🛒 ✗ 🛒 🏠 M 🏛 ❀ ≋ ⛲ 🏖 🚗 🚌
Washing sinks. Restaurant, food to order. Internet 10Dh/hr.	All 1km in Zagora.

🚐+🚹🚺= 60Dh   **All Year**   ⛺+🚹🚺= 40Dh

ZAGORA | 122 | E5

Camping L'Oasis Enchantée, Aroumiate, Zagora.
Tel: 0662 781984 www.oasis-enchantee.com

GB F D   E I   CC €

A small and peaceful campsite shaded by palm trees. Pitches are partially marked, the surfaces being stones, sand and grass. Facilities appeared clean and well maintained. At the time of inspection (2009) this was the only campsite in Zagora with a swimming pool. Onsite restaurant makes meals to order. 4x4 and camel trips can be organised.

Pitch No:	Water:		Electric:			Disposal Details (sanitation):			
9	⚱	Dh	E	Amp	Dh		MB	MG	🚽 In toilet.

Toilets:	No.	No.				Showers:	No.	No.		
WC	♂6	♀6	S	C		🚿	♂4	♀4	H	Dh
Unisex.						Unisex.				

Directions: Just off the N9 2km north of Zagora. Well signed off the road to the left, follow the track as signed for 400m.

GPS: N30°22.313' W005°50.442'

Campsite Amenities:	Local Amenities Nearby (5km or less):
Washing sinks. Swimming pool summer only.	All 2km in Zagora.

 = 60Dh | **All Year** |  = 55Dh

MOROCCO   MAROC

Camping de la Palmeraie D'Amezrou, Amezrou, Zagora.
Tel: 0667 596289

A popular campsite located in the palmerai. Tall palm trees provide plenty of shade and the partially marked pitches are mainly on firm sand. Facilities were clean and well maintained. A kitchen is available for clients' use. The restaurant makes Moroccan meals to order, which can be served on the terrace or in a nomad tent. Tented accommodation is also available. Camel and 4x4 trips can be organised.

Pitch No:	Water:			Electric:			Disposal Details (sanitation):				
40			Dh	E	Amp	15Dh		MB	MG		

Toilets:	No.	No.			Showers:	No.	No.		
WC	♦2	♦2	S	C		♦3	♦3	H	10Dh

Directions: Located south of Zagora. From the north drive through the town centre. After crossing the bridge take the track to the right, signed 'camping', just before the right hand bend. Drive 200m alongside the water channel to the campsite.

GPS: N30°18.891' W005°49.773'

Campsite Amenities:	Local Amenities Nearby (5km or less):
Cold water sinks.	All 1.5km in Zagora.

+♦♦= 40Dh   **All Year**   **+♦♦= 30Dh**

OULED DRISS 124 E6

Camping Kasbah Ouled Driss, Mhamid 45400 Zagora.
Tel: 0524 848691

GB F D E I CC €

Refreshingly green, this pleasant campsite is close to the centre of the old desert village. Pitches are mainly unmarked on firm sand. The facilities were clean and well maintained. Moroccan meals ordered from the restaurant can be served inside or on the covered terrace. Tented accommodation and rooms are available, for example: full board double room, 250Dh. Camel and 4x4 trips can be organised.

Pitch No:	Water:			Electric:			Disposal Details (sanitation):			
24	🦽		Dh	E	Amp	Dh	▥	MB	MG	🛗

Toilets:	No.	No.				Showers:	No.	No.			
WC	♂4	♀4	S	C		♨	♂6	♀6	H		10Dh
Unisex.						Unisex.					

Directions: On the N9 Zagora to Mhamid road, signed in the middle of the village.

GPS: N29°49.768' W005°39.319'

Campsite Amenities:	Local Amenities Nearby (5km or less):
⏺ 💈 ⚒ ✂ ✗ ⓘ WD	🍴 ✗ 🛒 🏠 🏛 M 🏰 🚲 〰 🔍 🏖 🚗 🚌
Cold water sinks. Internet included.	All 100m in village.

MOROCCO   MAROC

Camping Nomade Paradise Garden, BP7, 45400 Bonu-Mhamid Ghizlan.
Tel: 0666 716856 www.paradise-garden-maroc.com

Ⅹ ⬜ ⬜ ⬜ ⬜ ⬜

⬜ ⬜ ⬜ ⬜ ⬜ ⬜ ⬜ ♪ GB F D E I NL CC €

Dutch owned, this is a large sandy campsite with little shade. On arrival visitors are given a useful information sheet about the site. The pitches are mainly unmarked and mostly on firm sand. Facilities are modern, clean and well maintained. The swimming pool is open all year. Moroccan meals are available to order and can be served inside the tented restaurant or on the covered terrace. Tented accommodation is available from 60Dh per person. Camel and 4x4 trips can be organised.

Pitch No:	Water:		Electric:			Disposal Details (sanitation):				
60	🚰	✂ Dh	E	Amp	15Dh	IIII	MB	MG	⬜	⬜
						Via manhole in drive.				

Toilets:	No.	No.				Showers:	No.	No.		
WC	🚹 10	🚻 10	S	C	♿	🚿	🚹 10	🚻 10	H ❄	10Dh
Unisex.						Unisex.				

Directions: On the N9 Zagora to Mhamid road, 4km before Mhamid, signed.

GPS: N29°49.631' W005°40.913'

Campsite Amenities:	Local Amenities Nearby (5km or less):
🔲 🍖 ⬜ ⚓ ✗ ⓘ WiFi	🔲 ✗ 🛒 ⬜ 🏛 M 🏰 ⬜ ≋ ⬜ 🏖 🚗 🚌
Cold water sinks. Bread to order.	All 1km in village.
Swimming pool 35Dh. Internet 15Dh/hr.	

⬜+🚹🚻= 45Dh   **All Year**   Ⅹ+🚹🚻= 40Dh

Camping Hamada du Draa, BP15, Mhamid 45400.
Tel: 0524 848086 www.hamada-sahara.com

GB F E I €

Right at the end of the tarmac road, only 4x4s and camels venture beyond this campsite! A high wall encloses the site. Firm sandy pitches are partially marked by stones and small trees or bushes. Only partial shade is available and an onsite hammam is available. Meals are cooked to order and can be eaten in the restaurant or outside. Various standards of accommodation. 4x4 and camel trips can be organised.

Pitch No:	Water:	Electric:	Disposal Details (sanitation):
50	Drinking water available at marked taps.	**E** **15Dh**	MG

Toilets: No.	No.		Showers: No.	No.
WC Ť2	Ť2 **S**		Ť2	Ť2 **H**
Unisex.				

Directions: Follow the road into the village and turn left in the centre at the roundabout. The site is straight ahead across the Oued.

GPS: N29°49.282' W005°43.245'

Campsite Amenities:	Local Amenities Nearby (5km or less):
Washing machine 30Dh. Swimming pool summer only. Internet 10Dh/hr.	**M** Market (souk) Monday. All in village.

+Ťᵗ= 40Dh   **All Year**   **+Ťᵗ= 40Dh**

MOROCCO   MAROC

Camping Auberge Ouadjou, N'kob, Zagora.
Tel: 0524 839314 www.ouadjou.com

A courtyard campsite that is small and pleasant. The high quality facilities are kept clean. The campsite entrance is tight 3m maximum width. The ground is all gravelled and pitches are unmarked. There are two large bays for motorhomes and another area for 4x4s or tents. Accommodation is available in the Auberge or nomad tents. Meals are available to order, and site owners will buy basic groceries for you upon request. N'kob is a centre for trekking or 4x4 expeditions in the Jbel Sahro and the Auberge has an experienced guide available.

Pitch No:	Water:	Electric:	Disposal Details (sanitation):
8 motorhomes **8** 4x4	Dh	**E** Amp **15Dh**	

Toilets: No. No.	Showers: No. No.
WC ♦2 ♦2 S C	♦2 ♦2 **H** Dh
Unisex.	Unisex.

Directions: On the R108. On the right just as you enter the town from the west.

GPS: N30°52.083' W005°52.107'

Campsite Amenities:
Swimming pool summer only 40Dh.
WiFi planned.

Local Amenities Nearby (5km or less):
All 1km in N'kob.

+♦♦= 55Dh   **All Year**   **+♦♦= 55Dh**

MAROC

MOROCCO

Camping Caravanning International Amrhidil, Skoura.
Tel: 0524 852328 www.camping-skoura-maroc.com

⛺ 🚐 🚐 🚐 🚌 🚐

🚐 🚐 ▦ ▦ SP 🏴 🔥 ♨ ♫ GB **F** D E I CC €

Close to the Amrhidil Kasbah, this family run, walled campsite is relatively new but somewhat rustic. Pitches are surfaced with hard sand and gravel. A wood fired boiler provides hot water for showers, you may need to order hot water in advance! A small restaurant serves traditional Moroccan dishes to order. Access may be difficult in wet weather because of the adjacent Oued.

Pitch No:	Water:			Electric:			Disposal Details (sanitation):			
40	🔧	▨ Dh		**E**	Amp	**15Dh**	▥	MB	MG	🏚
										10Dh.

Toilets:	No.	No.	No.	No.		Showers:	No.	No.		
WC	🚹 4	🚺 4	**S**	**C**	♿	🚿	🚹 2	🚺 1	**H**	❄ 10Dh
Unisex.										

Directions: Coming from Ouarzazate the site is signed on the left just before the start of Skoura and is about 300m down the track, follow signs. Access may be difficult in wet weather because of the adjacent Oued.

GPS: N31°02.975' W006°34.590'

Campsite Amenities:	Local Amenities Nearby (5km or less):
🔲 🍴 ⚒ ✗ ✗ ① WiFi	🛒 ✗ 🛒 🏛 🏠 M 🏰 ⚙ ≋ ⛽ ⛵ 🚐 🚌
Cold water sinks.	All in town about 1km. Tourist attraction Kasbah 300m.

🚐+🚹🚺= **30Dh**   **All Year**   ⛺+🚹🚺= **30Dh**

Hotel Camping Soleil Bleu, BP23 Boumalne Dadès, Ouarzazate.
Tel: 0524 830163 www.hotelsoleilbleu.com

GB F D E I   CC €

The bare parking is in a high walled courtyard alongside the hotel. There are good views over the town and valley from one end and the facilities are excellent. A guide is available for tours of the gorges and mountains around the area. On Wednesday a souk is held nearby.

Pitch No:	Water:			Electric:			Disposal Details (sanitation):				
20		Dh		E	Amp	20Dh		MB	MG		

Toilets:	No.	No.	No.	No.		Showers:	No.	No.		
WC	♂ 2	♂ 2	S	C			♂ 2	♂ 2	H	10Dh
Unisex.						Unisex.				

Directions: Take the road alongside the fuel station at the eastern edge of the town, well signed.

GPS: N31°22.580' W005°58.875'

Campsite Amenities:	Local Amenities Nearby (5km or less):

All in town 2km. Market (souk) 500m.

🚐+♂♀= 40Dh   **All Year**   ⛺+♂♀= 30Dh

MAROC

MOROCCO

BOUMALNE DADES (Gorges du Dadès) `130` **D6**

Camping Ait Oudinar, BP95 Boumalne Dadès, Ouarzazate.
Tel: 0524 830221 www.aubergeaitoudinar.com

△ 🚐 🚗 🚙 🚌 🚃

🚐 🚐 〰 ▦ SP ▨ 🔒 🧴 ♫ **GB F** D E I CC €

Amongst trees on the edge of the river this is an attractive campsite split on two levels, one of which is above flood level. The ground is part gravelled and the pitches are unmarked. A small grass area is set aside for tents. There is a restaurant in the Auberge and a terrace with views across the valley. A room furnished with tables and couches is also available. Cycle hire, 4x4 trips, and guides are available.

Pitch No:	Water:			Electric:			Disposal Details (sanitation):			
35	🚰	✕	Dh	**E**	Amp	Dh	▥	MB	MG	🔲 In toilet.

Toilets:	No.	No.	No.	No.		Showers:	No.	No.		
WC Unisex.	👤3	👤3	**S**	**C** ♿		🚿 Unisex.	👤3	👤3	**H** ❄	Dh

Directions: About 22km from Boumalne Dadès on the R704 road up the gorge.

GPS: N31°30.331' W005°56.699'

Campsite Amenities:
▣ 🛒 ♨ ✕ ⓘ WiFi
Washing machine 20Dh. Internet 10Dh/hr.

Local Amenities Nearby (5km or less):
🏧 ✕ 🛒 🏦 ▦ Ⓜ 🏰 🚲 ≋ ⚓ 🏕 🚐 🚌
Tourist attraction adjacent.

🚐+👤👤= 45Dh **All Year** △+👤👤= 30Dh

125

BOUMALNE DADES (Gorges du Dadès)   131   D6

Hotel Camping Berbere de la Montagne, Boumalne Dadès, Ouarzazate.
Tel: 0524 830228   www.berbere-montagne.ift.fr

GB F D E I CC €

This campsite is well situated immediately after the narrowest parts of the gorge making it a good base for exploring the area. The site is flat and part gravelled with unmarked pitches. The modern facilities are kept clean but there is no toilet cassette emptying facility. The Auberge has a restaurant.

Pitch No:	Water:			Electric:			Disposal Details (sanitation):				
30			Dh	E	Amp	15Dh		MB	MG		

Toilets:	No.	No.	No.	No.		Showers:	No.	No.			
WC	♂ 2	♀ 2	S	C	♿		♂ 3	♀ 3	H	❄	Dh
Unisex.						Unisex.					

Directions: About 34km from Boumalne Dadès on the R704 road up the gorge.

GPS: N31°33.453' W005°54.564'

Campsite Amenities:

Local Amenities Nearby (5km or less):

Tourist attraction adjacent.

🚐 + ♂♀ = 60Dh	**All Year**	⛺ + ♂♀ = 45Dh

TINERHIR (Gorges du Todra) 132 D6

Auberge Camping Atlas, BP296 Tinerhir.
Tel: 0524 895046

GB F D E I CC €

A nice, small campsite opposite a palmerai on the edge of the river but is well above flood level. There is direct access by footbridge across the river to the palmerai making this a good base for walking in the valley. Facilities were very clean and well maintained. There is an attractive restaurant with terrace and tented eating areas.

Pitch No:	Water:			Electric:		Disposal Details (sanitation):				
24	⚱	✗	Dh	**E**	Amp **15Dh**	▥	MB	**MG**	🚪	

Toilets:	No.	No.	No.	No.		Showers:	No.	No.			
WC	⚲3	⚲3	**S**	**C**	♿	☂	⚲4	⚲4	**H**	❄	Dh
Unisex.						Unisex.					

Directions: Take the road signed 'Gorges du Todra' in Tinerhir. The site is on the right in about 10km. Warning, steep entry.

GPS: N31°33.184' W005°35.129'

Campsite Amenities:
Washing machine 30Dh.
Swimming pool at hotel.

Local Amenities Nearby (5km or less):

🚐+⚲⚲= 40Dh   **All Year**   ⛺+⚲⚲= 35Dh

TINERHIR (Gorges du Todra)   133   D6

Hotel-Camping Le Soleil, 45800 Tinerhir, Maroc.
Tel: 0524 895111 www.hotelcampinglesoleil.com

GB F D E I   CC €

This campsite is well kept with facilities that are up to European standards. Trees and bushes mark the pitches and also provide plenty of shade. There is a good restaurant, and an open all year swimming pool. This site is popular with tour groups and makes a good base from which to visit the gorge 7km away. On Mondays there is a souk in Tinerhir.

Pitch No:	Water:			Electric:			Disposal Details (sanitation):				
60		Dh		E	Amp	20Dh	IIII	MB	MG		

Toilets:	No.	No.	No.	No.		Showers:	No.	No.		
WC	♂9	♀9	S	C		♀9	♂9	H		Dh
Unisex.						Unisex.				

Directions: Take the road signed 'Gorges du Todra' in Tinerhir. The site is on the left in about 8km.

GPS: N31°32.853' W005°35.416'

Campsite Amenities: Local Amenities Nearby (5km or less):
Washing machine 25Dh. WiFi planned.

⊞+♂♀= 50Dh   **All Year**   **⚠+♂♀= 45Dh**

Camping les Tamaris, Avenue Hassan II, 52250 Goulmima.
Tel: 0535 885413 www.chez-michele.com/le_camping_des_tamaris-en.htm

This campsite was the old town Municipal Camping site. This site is gradually being refurbished but looked a little unkempt on entering. The ample sized motorhome pitches are nicely laid out and well marked by small trees and bushes. Facilities were old but well kept and very clean. Drinking water from marked taps only. Unusually there is a charge for both hot and cold showers. Restaurant meals cooked to order. A pool is available in summer.

Pitch No:	Water:		Electric:		Disposal Details (sanitation):			
20 (100)	⚲	**10Dh**	**E** Amp	**15Dh**			🗲 In toilet.	

Toilets:	No.	No.	No.	No.	Showers: No.	No.		
WC Unisex.	🕇 11	🕇 11	**S**	**C**	🕭 🕇 3	🕇 3	**H** ❄	**5/10Dh**
					Cold 5Dh, hot 10Dh. Unisex.			

Directions: Near the centre of the town, behind the bus station (Gare Routiere), well signed.

GPS: N31°41.187' W004°57.504'

Campsite Amenities:　　　　　　Local Amenities Nearby (5km or less):

Washing machine 20Dh.　　　　　All in town a few hundred metres.

🚐+🕇🕇= 35Dh　　　　　　**All Year**　　　　　　Λ+🕇🕇= 30Dh

MERZOUGA   🔔   **135**   E7

Auberge Camping La Tradition, Village Merzouga Par Rissani, Ar-Rachidia.
Tel: 0670 039244

▲ 🚐 🚐 🚐 🚌 🚐

🚐 🚐 〜 ▓ SP 📷 🍶 🎵   GB F D E I   CC €

Just one of many campings signed in the area but this site has the advantage of being right at the base of the dunes, and the disadvantage that it has very little shade, or shelter from the wind. Facilities were rather limited at the time of our visit, but a new sanitary block was under construction. Meals are available to order in the Auberge restaurant. As with all similar establishments in the area, camel and 4x4 trips can be organised. Overnight trips allow tourists to spend some time with nomad families and to see the Sahara sunrise.

Pitch No:	Water:	No.	No.	Electric:			Disposal Details (sanitation):				
50	🚰	✗	Dh	**E**	Amp	Dh	▥	MB	MG	🚽	🚐

Toilets:	No.	No.	No.	No.	Showers:	No.	No.			
WC 👨2	👩2	S	**C**	♿	🚿 👨2	👩2	**H**	❄	Dh
Unisex.					Unisex.				

Directions: At the foot of Erg Chebbi, just before Merzouga turn right, signed for Taouz. The site is off the road to the left, signed, in around 1km.

GPS: N31°05.060' W004°00.429'

Campsite Amenities:	Local Amenities Nearby (5km or less):
📷 🏛 🍷 ✗ ⓘ WiFi	🍴 ✗ 🛒 🕌 ▥ **M** 🏰 🌿 〜 🔍 🏖 🚗 🚌
	All in Merzouga 1km.

🚐 + 👨👩 = 30Dh   **All Year**   ▲ + 👨👩 = 30Dh

Camping Tifina, BP204 Erfoud 52200, Ar-Rachidia.
Tel: 0610 231414 www.tifina-maroc.com

GB F D E I   CC €

A new campsite that was under construction in February 2009. According to the owner, works will be completed in 2009 and it will be a first class campsite, among the best in Morocco. Pitches are a good size and well marked by small hedges. Completed facilities were excellent. Prices are staged according to the level of services provided: Premium, inc hot shower, 80Dh. Comfort, inc hot shower and electric hook-up, 110Dh. Luxe, electric hook-up and private bathroom with hot shower, basin and toilet, 210Dh. Various classes of accommodation are also available from 100Dh to 310Dh per person. A motorhome service and washing area is provided but the cassette emptying point was rudimentary. Separate bins are provided for rubbish recycling. Hammam available, Jacuzzi available in summer. Camel and 4x4 trips to Erg Chebbi can be organised.

Pitch No:	Water:			Electric:			Disposal Details (sanitation):				
90	Inc.		Dh	**E**	Amp	**20Dh**		MB	MG		
				Included on higher tariffs.							

Toilets: No.	No.	No.	No.		Showers: No.	No.		
WC ♂ 4	♀ 4	S	C	♿	♂ 5	♀ 5	H	Dh
					Included on higher tariffs.			

Directions: On the N13 from Rissani to Erfoud around 8km south of Erfoud.

GPS: N31°23.037' W004°16.327'

Campsite Amenities:
Washing machine 60Dh. Swimming pool summer only.

Local Amenities Nearby (5km or less):

🚐+♂♀= 80Dh   **All Year**   ⛺+♂♀= 80Dh

AR-RACHIDIA 137 D7

Camping Tissirt, Route d'Erfoud, Ar-Rachidia.
Tel: 0662 141378

SP GB F D E I CC €

A small campsite located in the palmerai. A steep track and sharp bend makes access difficult for large motorhomes. Facilities, though not modern, are clean and well maintained, also there is a small campers kitchen. Defined pitches are mostly on firm, bare ground. The site is a good base from which to explore the Gorges du Ziz.

Pitch No:	Water:	Electric:	Disposal Details (sanitation):
16	20Dh	E Amp 15Dh	MB MG

Toilets:	No.	No.	No.	No.	Showers:	No.	No.		
WC	2	2	S	C		2	2	H	Dh

Directions: 30 km south of Ar Rachidia on the N13 to Erfoud, signed down a steep track.

GPS: N31°47.062' W004°13.825'

Campsite Amenities: WiFi
Washing service.

Local Amenities Nearby (5km or less): M
Shop in village 1km. Public transport on main road.

+ = 50Dh | All Year | + = 45Dh

AR-RACHIDIA   138   D7

Camping Source Bleue de Meski, Meski, Ar-Rachidia.

GB F D E I CC €

A pleasant site in a small palmerai alongside a natural spring fed stream, which is channelled into a swimming pool. The palms provide plenty of shade. The pitches are unmarked and the site is quiet in winter as long as a tour group is not visiting. Run by the local community, profits from the site go to help the village. Unusually the site has souvenir and artefact shops within it and there is a little good-humoured hassling from the traders. The showers seem to be run as a separate enterprise and their guardian doesn't keep them clean and toilets are no better. Drinking water is from marked taps only. Café/restaurant cooks meals to order. Good base for visiting the ruined ksar on the opposite bank of the river, or for a trek down the Ziz valley.

Pitch No:	Water:			Electric:			Disposal Details (sanitation):			
60	🚰		Dh	**E**	Amp	Dh		MB	MG	

Toilets:	No.		No.		No.		No.	Showers:	No.		No.			
WC	5		5	**S**	**C**				1		1	**H**		**10Dh**
Unisex.								Unisex.						

Directions: N13 Ar Rachidia - Erfoud. About 24km south of Ar Rachidia, on the N13 take the turning signed to the campsite. The campsite is on the right in a few hundred metres, through the large pillars. Drivers of large motorhomes must stop and walk to the entrance to confirm access is possible.
GPS: N31°51.526' W004°16.988'

Campsite Amenities:

Local Amenities Nearby (5km or less):

Shop and restaurant in village 500m. Public transport at main road junction, 1km.

🚐+👫= 40Dh   **All Year**   ⛺+👫= 35Dh

Camping Municipal, Midelt.

This old Municipal Camping was undergoing refurbishment when we visited in March 2009. Hard standing pitches are being provided along with a new reception, restaurant and sanitary block. Each pitch will have individual water and electric points. A motorhome service point is also being constructed. Works were expected to be completed in May 2009 and from what we saw this should result in a good quality site. The price will increase once the site is fully open.

Pitch No:	Water:			Electric:			Disposal Details (sanitation):				
40	🚰		Dh	E	Amp	Dh	IIII	MB	MG		Planned.
				tba							

Toilets:	No.	No.	No.	No.		Showers:	No.	No.			
WC	� 4	♯ 4	S	C	♿	🚿	♯ 4	♯ 4	H	❄	Dh
						Cost unknown.					

Directions: Signed off the main road in the town, the site is located behind the Hotel Ayachi next to the old Municipal Stadium.

GPS: N32°40.617' W004°44.273'

Campsite Amenities:

Cold water sinks.

Local Amenities Nearby (5km or less):

All in town approx 500m.

🚐+♯♯= 25Dh   **All Year**   ⛺+♯♯= 20Dh

MAROC
MOROCCO

Timnay Inter-Cultural Complexe Touristique, BP81 Midelt 54350.
Tel: 0535 583434

GB F CC €

This is a popular trans-Morocco 4x4 and tour stop at a tourist centre with restaurant, swimming pool and rooms. The riad is undergoing restoration and will be open to visitors on completion. Camping pitches are on grass, situated between rows of pine trees providing plenty of shade. Additional pitches were being constructed, along with a second sanitary block with washing machines. The centre organises 4x4 tours and can give advice on routes, also they will provide a recovery service if necessary! A repair workshop and tools are available for hire and the services of a local mechanic can be obtained if required.

Pitch No:	Water:	No.	Dh	Electric:	Amp	15Dh	Disposal Details (sanitation):				
70				E				MB	MG		

Toilets:	No.	No.	No.	No.	Showers:	No.	No.		
WC	♂5	♀5	S	C		♂3	♀3	H	Dh

Directions: On the N13 about 21km north of Midelt.

GPS: N32°45.148' W004°55.191'

Campsite Amenities:

Local Amenities Nearby (5km or less):

Swimming pool summer only.

🚐+♂♀= 61Dh **All Year** ⛺+♂♀= 51Dh

TIMAHDITE   142   C6

Auberge Camping du Col du Zad, Timahdite.
Tel: 0612 162076

Camping on terraced pitches alongside the Auberge. The ground was very soft and inaccessible due to snowdrifts when we visited in mid March 2009. Hard standing parking was possible in front of the Auberge. Toilet and shower block access was virtually blocked by snow and the facilities had not been in use for some time. Although claimed to be open all year this site is at over 2000m in the Middle Atlas and access may be difficult or impossible at times during the winter.

Pitch No:	Water:	No.	Dh	Electric:	Amp	Dh	Disposal Details (sanitation):				
100				**E** Generator.						In toilet.	

Toilets:	No.	No.	No.	No.		Showers:	No.	No.			
WC ♂4	♀4	S	C			♂2	♀2	H		Dh	
Unisex.						Unisex.					

Directions: On the N13 Azrou to Midelt road, a few km north of the Col du Zad pass.

GPS: N33°03.500' W005°02.289'

Campsite Amenities: Local Amenities Nearby (5km or less):

Washing machine inc.

🚐+♂♀= 100Dh   **All Year**   ⛺+♂♀= 100Dh

MAROC   # MOROCCO

Camping Zebra, BP 747, 22000 Azilal.
Tel: 0666 328576 www.gewoongaan.nl

GB F D E I CC €

Dutch owned and laid back this small campsite was opened in 2008. Pitches are terraced, most providing superb views across the valley. Facilities are somewhat rustic, but clean. This site is 1.5km from the cascades at Ouzoud.

Pitch No:	Water:		Electric:		Disposal Details (sanitation):	
20	🚿 Dh		E Amp	15Dh		🔲

Toilets:	No.	No.	No.	No.	Showers:	No.	No.		
WC	♂1	♀1	S	C	👁	♂2	♀2	H ❄	Dh
Unisex.					Unisex, one hot one cold.				

Directions: Take the road signed Cascades d'Ouzoud off the R304. The site is on the right, just before the village of Ouzoud, signed.

GPS: N32°00.529' W006°43.157'

Campsite Amenities:	Local Amenities Nearby (5km or less):
🍴 ✕	🛒 ✕
Cold water sinks.	All 1.5km in Ouzoud.

🚐+♂♀= 50Dh   **All Year**   ⛺+♂♀= 50Dh

CASCADES D'OUZOUD `146` D5

Camping Amalou.

Located in a grassy olive grove, this is a basic but level campsite that is only few hundred metres away from the waterfall. Access to the campsite is weather dependant as it may be muddy or flooded after heavy rain. The facilities were dilapidated and dirty. Other parking possibilities in the village are: the sloping parking area in the centre (10Dh/day, 20Dh/night), a flat parking area behind the Gendarmerie (40Dh/night) and Camping de la Nature behind Riad du Cascades which is really only suitable for tents.

Pitch No:	Water:			Electric:			Disposal Details (sanitation):				
50	🚰	✄	Dh	**E**	Amp	**10Dh**	▥	MB	MG	⌑	▤

Toilets:	No.	No.	No.	No.		Showers:	No.	No.			
WC	♂ 1	♀ 1	S	**C**	♿	🚿	♂ 1	♀ 1	H	❄	Dh

Directions: Take the road signed Cascades d'Ouzoud off the R304. Go into the village of Ouzoud, the site is on the left after going round the sharp right hand bend, signed.

GPS: N32°00.817' W006°43.058'

Campsite Amenities:	Local Amenities Nearby (5km or less):
📷 🍴 ✕ ⓘ WiFi	🛒 ✕ 🏠 Ⓜ 🏰 ≈ 🚌
Café in summer.	All 200m in village.

 🚐+♂♀= 40Dh   **All Year**   ⚊+♂♀= 30Dh

MAROC   MOROCCO

Euro Camping, Emirates Tourist Center, Azrou.
Tel: 0613 143030 www.camping-morocco.com

This was a new site under construction as part of a large tourist complex, known locally as 'Disneyland'. We were unable to obtain details, as the site was not open in early March 2009.

Pitch No:	Water:		Electric:		Disposal Details (sanitation):			
	Dh		E Amp Dh			MB	MG	

Toilets:	No.	No.	No.	No.	Showers: No.	No.			
			S C					H	Dh

Directions: Alongside the Azrou - Ifrane road, 4km from Azrou.

GPS: N33°26.691' W005°11.476'

Campsite Amenities: Local Amenities Nearby (5km or less):

+ = Unknown   **All Year**   + = Unknown

MOROCCO   MAROC

Camping Amazigh, BP136, Azrou 53100.
Tel: 0665 361640 www.campingamazigh.com

GB F D E **CC €**

A very attractive campsite set amongst ancient cherry trees. Facilities are clean and well kept. A wood-burning boiler heats water for the showers so you may have to request that it is lit! Unusually the site has separate bins for recycling rubbish. Home cooked traditional Moroccan food is available on request.

Pitch No:	Water:			Electric:			Disposal Details (sanitation):			
40 (20)		Dh		**E**	Amp	**20Dh**		MG		

Toilets:	No.	No.	No.	No.		Showers:	No.	No.		
WC	♂ 4	♀ 4	S	C			♂ 6	♀ 6	H	Dh

Directions: Alongside the Azrou - Ifrane road, 5km from Azrou, signed.

GPS: N33°26.959' W005°10.235'

Campsite Amenities:	Local Amenities Nearby (5km or less):
Washing machine 30Dh. Shop summer only.	All 5km in Azrou.

+ ♂♀ = 50Dh   **All Year**   **+ ♂♀ = 50Dh**

Camping Caravaneserai, Rue Sidi Ali Boussarghine, Sefrou.
Tel: 0535 662165

This campsite is set high above Sefrou and has far-reaching views over the town and surrounding countryside. In fact the views were the only appealing feature in January 2009 as work was going on in various parts of the site, presumably to improve the run down facilities. Sadly the site guardian had little interest in explaining what was going on so we had no idea what was planned or when it might be completed. The one sanitary block in use had three toilets that looked newly installed and three cold showers but there was evidence of a gas boiler installation. The site, set amongst pine trees, is terraced, some providing gravel hard standing and some providing grass for tents.

Pitch No:	Water:			Electric:			Disposal Details (sanitation):				
50				**E**						🚽 In toilet	

Toilets:	No.	No.	No.	No.	Showers:	No.	No.			
🚹 WC Unisex.	♂ 3	♂ 3	S			🚿 Unisex.	♂ 3	♂ 3	H	❄️

Directions: In Sefrou town centre look for the 'Camping Municipal' signs at the traffic lights. Go up the road (Sidi Ali Boussarghine), the site is in around 2km, you have to make a short right - left - left - right detour round a one way system just before you get there.

GPS: N33°49.212' W004°50.573'

Campsite Amenities:
Cold water sinks.

Local Amenities Nearby (5km or less):
All 2km in town.

🚐 + ♂♀ = 50Dh   **All Year**   ⛺ + ♂♀ = 50Dh

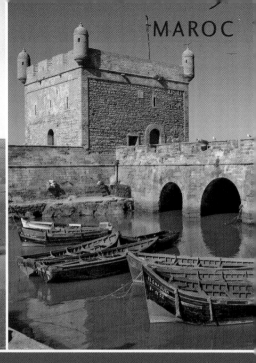

THE FOLLOWING LISTINGS ARE CONVENIENT
OVERNIGHT STOPS OR HAVE LIMITED FACILITIES

OUEZZANE 8 B6

Motel Rif Aire de Repos, Route de Fès, Bni Kola, Ouezzane.
Tel: 0537 907172 www.motel-rif.ma

This small rest area is located alongside the main road. This is a useful overnight service stop that has parking for about 30 motorhomes. The small, immaculately kept sanitary block with toilet and bidet block also has a large shower room. Organic produce from the nearby farm is available and is also served in the onsite restaurant.

Pitch No:	Water:		Electric:			Disposal Details (sanitation):				
30	🚰	Dh	E	Amp	Dh		MB	MG	🚪	

Toilets:	No.	No.				Showers:	No.	No.		
WC	♂1	♀1	S	C	♿	🚿	♂1	♀1	H	Dh
Unisex.						Unisex.				

Directions: About 3km south of Ouezzane on the road to Fès/Meknès, signed.

GPS: N34°46.375' W005°32.718'

Campsite Amenities:

Swimming pool summer only.

Local Amenities Nearby (5km or less):

M

All 3km at Ouezzane.

🚐+♂♀= 50Dh   **All Year**   ⛺+♂♀= N/A

CABO NEGRO   12   B6

Complexe La Ferma, BP 16, M'Diq, par Tetouan 93200.
Tel: 0539 978075   www.laferma.com

The parking is alongside the attractive La Ferma hotel restaurant, which serves a range of traditional and modern Moroccan food. If you eat in the restaurant there is no charge for using the parking. Pitches are laid out on terraces and marked out with tyres. There is an equestrian centre alongside and a swimming pool is available in summer.

Pitch No:	Water:		Electric:			Disposal Details (sanitation):				
30		Dh	Amp	Dh			MB	MG		

Toilets:	No.	No.			Showers:	No.	No.			
WC			S	C					H	Dh

May use those in restaurant.

Directions: Just after M'Diq on the N13 Ceuta to Tetouan road turn left, signed, 'Cabo Negro', site is 1km on the right, signed.

GPS: N35°39.989' W005°18.414'

Campsite Amenities:

Local Amenities Nearby (5km or less):

All 3km in M'Diq.

+îî= 60Dh	All Year	Δ+îî= N/A

MAROC   MOROCCO

Centre d'Acceuil Comarit, Comarit, Larache.
Tel: 0539 521069

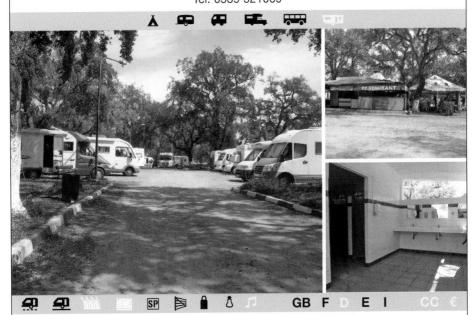

A large, busy area mostly shaded by mature trees. Parking is all on hard standing bays. Funded by the ferry company Comanav, use of the site is currently free but taking at least one meal in the restaurant is expected. This is no great hardship as meals are reasonably priced and the restaurant/café is open 24 hours. Camping fees are being considered for 2010. Facilities are good and kept very clean. As it is free and close to the ferry ports, this makes it very popular with motorhome travellers so may be crowded and noisy at times.

Pitch No:	Water:		Electric:		Disposal Details (sanitation):				
200									

Toilets: No.	No.			Showers: No.	No.		
6	6	S	C	2	2	H	

Directions: On the N1 towards Larache about 3 km after leaving the motorway junction.

GPS: N35°09.639' W006°08.582'

Campsite Amenities:	Local Amenities Nearby (5km or less):
Cold water sinks.	All in Larache. Bus stop outside.

+= Free   **All Year**   += Free

Centre d'Acceuil Comanav, Comanav, Larache.

This is a large open area with some shaded parking for cars and small vans. Facilities are basic but clean. Funded by the ferry company Comanav. Use of the site is free, but you should eat in the restaurant as a gesture of goodwill. It is located between the main road and the motorway so expect some road noise.

Pitch No:	Water:		Electric:			Disposal Details (sanitation):				
200		Dh	E Amp	Dh			MB	MG	In toilet	

Toilets:	No.	No.				Showers:	No.	No.			
WC	♀4	♂4	S	C			♀2	♂2	H		Dh

Directions: On the N1 towards Larache about 2 km after the motorway junction.

GPS: N35°08.905' W006°08.453'

Campsite Amenities:

Cold water sinks. Restaurant summer only.

Local Amenities Nearby (5km or less):

All in Larache 4km. Bus stop outside.

+♀♂ = Free   **All Year**   +♀♂ = Free

TLET BOUGUEDRA 49 D4

Aire de Repos Maison 234, Maison 234, Tlet Bouguedra, Province de Safi.
Tel: 0668 418197

GB F D E I CC €

Under development when visited in January 2009, and the facilities, whilst almost finished, could not be considered usable. If the plans come to fruition it will be a well-equipped motorhome stopover with marked parking bays towards the back of the site. Towards the front there will be a restaurant, shop and repair facilities.

Pitch No: 20

Water: Dh

Electric: E Amp 15Dh

Disposal Details (sanitation): MB MG

Toilets: WC No. 3 No. 3 S C
Unisex.

Showers: No. 1 No. 1 H 10Dh
Unisex.

Directions: On the N1 south of the crossroads with the R204, between Tlet Bouguedra and Sebt Gzoula.

GPS: N32°10.590' W009°02.359'

Campsite Amenities: WiFi
All available when/if development finished.

Local Amenities Nearby (5km or less): M

+ = 50Dh All Year + = 50Dh

Dar Ch'tis Halte Camping Cars, Sidi Kaouki, 44100, Essaouira.
Tel: 0672 675866

Brand new Aire de Stationnement for motorhomes only. All the individually marked bays are slightly sloping. The new sanitary block is top quality and was perfectly clean. Traditional Moroccan food is available to order.

Pitch No:	Water:		Electric:			Disposal Details (sanitation):				
18	🚰	Dh	E Amp	Dh		🗑	MB	MG		

Toilets:	No.	No.				Showers:	No.	No.		
WC	♂ 2	♀ 2	S	C	♿	🚿	♂ 2	♀ 2	H	Dh

Directions: South of Essaouira on the road to Agadir. Signed on the left about 1km past the turning to Sidi Kaouki. Site is down a 600m track through Argan trees.

GPS: N31°24.139' W009°42.595'

Campsite Amenities:

Local Amenities Nearby (5km or less):

🚐+♂♀= 80Dh **All Year** ▲+♂♀= N/A

TAMRHAKT 70 E3

Parking Camping Car Imourane.

GB F D

This newly approved overnight parking area opened following the closure of the campsite at Taghazoute and the subsequent demand for more motorhome parking places. Located right on the beach of the bay next to Banana Beach, facilities are limited, basic and dirty, nevertheless it is a very popular parking area. Beachside restaurants and surf centre nearby. This area was popular in 2009 with some people staying for weeks.

Pitch No: 150 | Water: | Electric: | Disposal Details (sanitation):

Toilets: WC No. 3 No. 3 C | Showers: No. 3 No. 3 5Dh

Directions: Parking Camping Car Imourane. About 10km north of Agadir, at Tamrhakt, signed towards the sea.

GPS: N30°36.614' W009°41.210'

Campsite Amenities:

Local Amenities Nearby (5km or less):

Shop and public transport 2km in village. Restaurant, day parking and beaches adjacent.

+ = 30Dh | All Year | + = N/A

Hotel-Camping Aglou Beach, Aglou Plage, Tiznit
Tel: 0528 866196

GB F D E I CC €

This flat parking area is in front of the hotel and adjacent to the beach. The surface is hard sand and gravel, but there are no marked bays. Dedicated toilets, clothes and dishwashing sinks are available. Hot showers in the hotel are available on request. There is a restaurant nearby. In 2009 this site was very popular with some people staying for weeks.

Pitch No:	Water:			Electric:			Disposal Details (sanitation):				
45	🚰	✗	Dh	E	Amp	Dh	⬛	MB	MG	🗄 In toliet.	

Toilets:	No.	No.			Showers:	No.	No.			
WC 👨2	👨2	S	C	♿	🚿 👨	👨	H	❄	12Dh
Unisex.					Showers in hotel.				

Directions: Carry on past the campsite Camping Aglou Plage, the parking is in front of the hotel on the right almost at the end of the road.

GPS: N29°48.247' W009°49.976'

Campsite Amenities:	Local Amenities Nearby (5km or less):
🔲 🧺 👕 ✂ ✗ ⓘ WiFi	🔧 ✗ 🛒 🏠 🏪 M 🏭 ♨ ≈ 🔍 🏖 ⛵ 🚌
Laundry service. Cold water sinks.	All within 200m.

🚐+👨👨= 30Dh   **All Year**   ⛺+👨👨= N/A

OFF-SITE PARKING

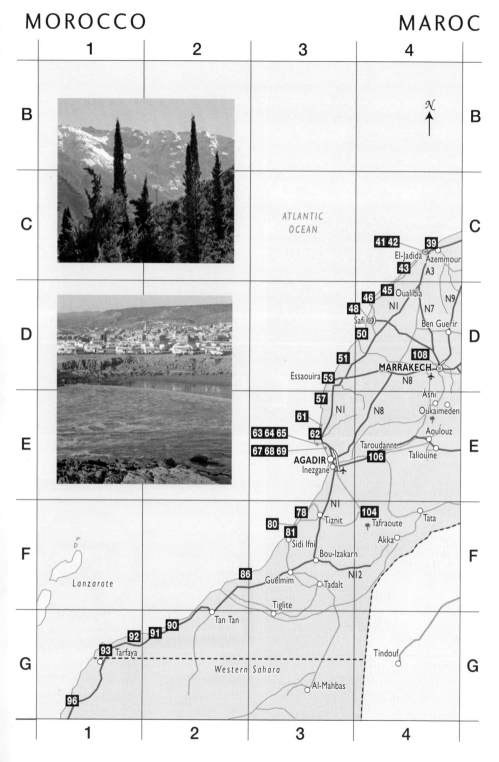

1   2   3   4

B   **B**

N

C   ATLANTIC   **C**
              OCEAN

41 42   **39**
                              El-Jadida Azemmour
                              43   A3

                              45 Oualidia
                         46   N9
                              N1   N7
                    48
                    Safi
D   **50**   Ben Guerir   **D**

                    51   **108**
          Essaouira **53**   MARRAKECH
                              N8
                    57
                    61   Asni
E   **63 64 65** **62** N1   N8   Oukaimeden   **E**
            67 68 69   Aoulouz
                    AGADIR   Taroudannt   Taliouine
                    Inezgane   **106**

                         N1
                    78   **104**   Tata
                80   Tiznit Tafraoute
F   **81**   Akka   **F**
                    Sidi Ifni
                         Bou-Izakarn
                    86   N12
          Lanzarote   Guelmim Tadalt
                         Tiglite
                         Tan Tan
                90
          92 91
G   **93** Tarfaya   Tindouf   **G**
                    Western Sahara

          96   Al-Mahbas

1   2   3   4

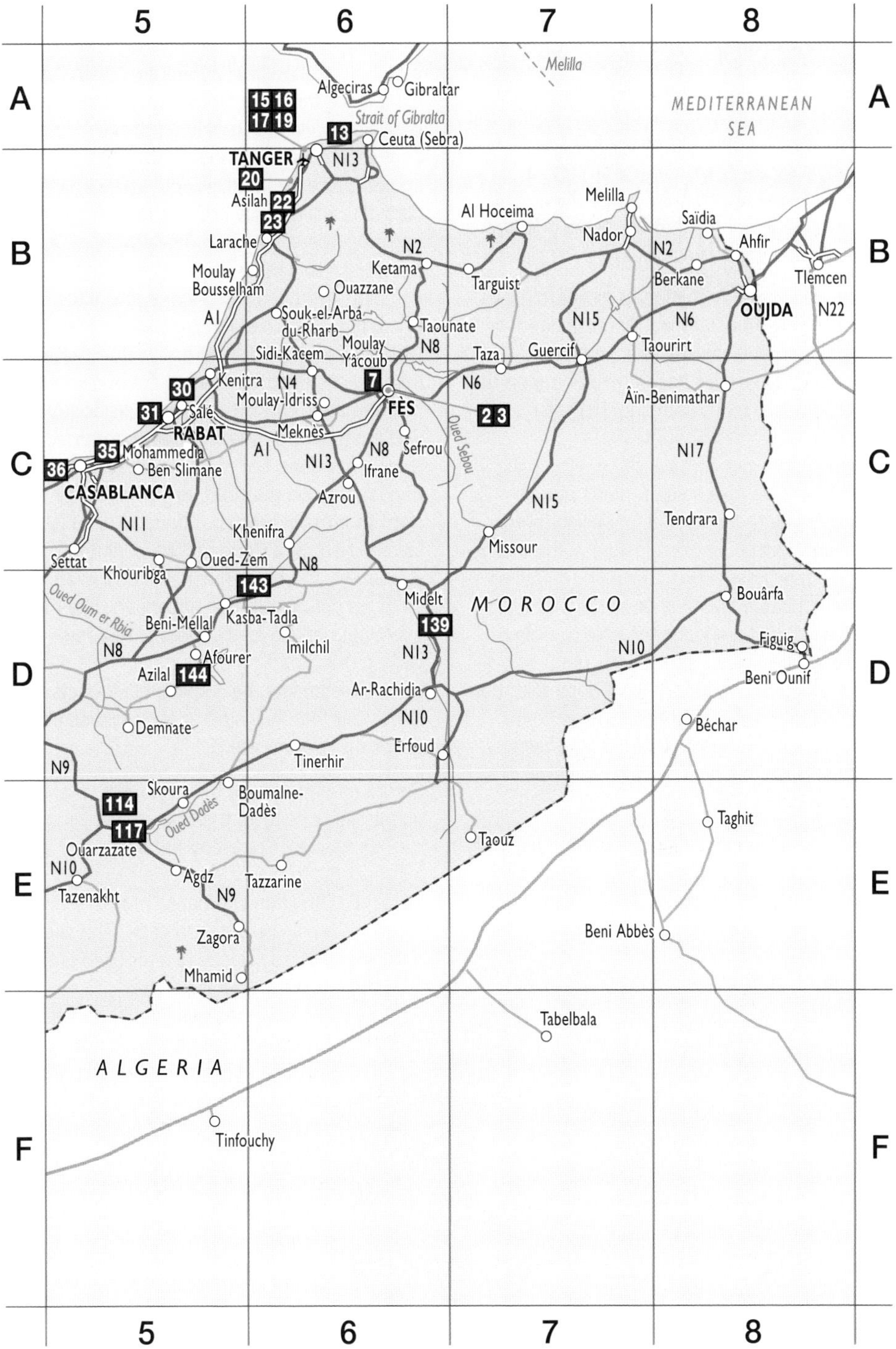

MAROC   MOROCCO

Map of Morocco with grid references. Place names and road numbers as labelled:

Grid columns 5, 6, 7, 8; Grid rows A, B, C, D, E, F

MEDITERRANEAN SEA

Melilla

Algeciras, Gibraltar, Strait of Gibraltar, Ceuta (Sebta)
15 16 17 19, **13**
TANGER **20**
Asilah **22**
23
Larache
Moulay Bousselham
Al Hoceima, Melilla, Saïdia, Ahfir, Tlemcen
Nador, Berkane, N2, N6, OUJDA, N22
Ketama, Targuist, N15
Ouazzane
Souk-el-Arbâ du-Rharb
Taounate, Taza, Guercif, Taourirt
Sidi-Kacem, Moulay Yâcoub, N8, N6
Kenitra, Moulay-Idriss, **30**
31 Salé, Meknès, **7** FÈS, **2 3**
RABAT, A1, N4
35 Mohammedia, N8, Sefrou, Âin-Benimathar
36 Ben Slimane, N13, Ifrane, N17
CASABLANCA, Azrou
N11, N15, Tendrara
Settat, Khenifra, Missour
Khouribga, Oued-Zem, N8
Oued Oum er Rbia
143 Midelt, MOROCCO, Bouârfa
Beni-Mellal, Kasba-Tadla, **139**, Figuig
N8, Afourer, Imilchil, N13, N10, Beni Ounif
Azilah, **144**, Ar-Rachidia, Béchar
Demnate, N10
N9, Erfoud
Tinerhir, Taghit
114 Skoura, Boumalne-Dadès
117 Oued Dadès
Ouarzazate, Taouz
N10, Agdz, Tazzarine, Beni Abbès
Tazenakht, N9
Zagora
Mhamid, Tabelbala
ALGERIA
Tinfouchy

Off-Site Parking

In addition to formal campsites, we have listed daytime parking locations for larger towns and beach surfing spots. Some are 'guarded parking' places where, for a small fee, a 'guardian' will 'watch-over your vehicle' but there is no guarantee that the same guardian will still be there on your return!

In the 'old-days', hundreds of motorhomers and campers free camped, unchallenged, in big gatherings along the Atlantic coast. Moroccan authorities have now put a stop to such unofficial mass camping; perhaps because of worries about crime, environmental concerns and the effects this would have on their valued tourist industry. Or possibly due to the actions of selfish motor caravanners that so often inspire authorities to act; we may never know. Despite contacting the Moroccan authorities on numerous occasions we have not been able to obtain the current rules and regulations regarding off-site parking. However, we have been told 'that you cannot camp anywhere you want: you should have the approval of the land owner and the government authorities or camp in an approved campsite'.

Despite the authorities stopping the mass free camping it is still possible to park at many town and beach car parks during the day.

Often by speaking to the guardian you will be told that you can park overnight, and in our experience this was perfectly safe. Generally overnight parking is restricted to self-contained (own toilet and waste facilities) campers and motorhomes but sometimes caravans will be allowed. This is parking not camping, therefore the use of awnings, barbeques or setting up camp with chairs or camping paraphernalia is not appropriate. Should you use these parking areas ensure you dispose of your toilet and water waste responsibly; and that doesn't mean down the nearest drain. **But be warned, just because you have paid a 'guardian' and obtained a 'receipt' it does not mean your vehicle will necessarily be guarded, or provide any right to stop overnight.** Where parking is located near to a Gendarmerie post it is courteous, and helps maintain good relations, if drivers check with the officers on duty that overnight parking is acceptable. Readers visiting these parking areas must make their own assessments, be responsible tourists and remember that they stop at such places at their own risk and liability.

Before off-site parking overnight get permission whenever possible and never park near campsites. Some say there is safety in numbers but in reality large groups attract unwanted attention and cause more

environmental damage. The sure-fire way to cause a problem is to outstay your welcome, motorhomes parking in one spot for weeks on end will alienate locals and officials. Off-site parking for a maximum of 48hrs will probably prevent ill feeling and should be more than enough time to explore the area. If you wish to stay longer, then book into a local campsite.

Liquid waste disposal - Where it is possible to empty waste tanks in an appropriate manner this has

been identified in the off-site parking entries. Do not simply pour toilet cassette contents down the nearest road drain, as this is irresponsible, illegal, and damaging to eco-systems. Morocco has a strong policy on responsible tourism and thoughtless waste disposal will only create ill feeling against campers. If you can find appropriate places to empty your waste water or toilet tanks responsibly, always clean up any mess. Leaving facilities cleaner than you found them will help promote a positive attitude towards campers. Campsites will sometimes let you service your camper for a small fee.

Change is inevitable and Morocco is developing quickly yet the old ways still dominate life. Expect things to change at short notice or without notice at all. It is quite likely that some of the parking places in this guide will no longer be as described or even available. Please let us know by filling in one of the report forms in the back of the guide, we also need to know if things stay the same.

Responsible Tourism

It is important to choose your stopping places carefully, adhere to any restrictions, and respect the local area. Tourist boards would prefer you to stop at campsites so when you are off-site parking do not set up camp for days on end, but stop only overnight. Putting out awnings and leaving collections of camping equipment out overnight is inappropriate. Everything should always be left exactly how it was found, if there is rubbish from previous users clearing this up will give locals a positive view of motorhomers. Where possible always use the official places, even if there is a charge this will encourage more to be set up, and support local communities. Never dispose of grey water or toilet waste into the environment, this is illegal, irresponsible, and could destroy a fragile ecosystem. When you travel you represent fellow motorhomers, fellow tourists, your country and mankind! Don't let them or us down.

MOROCCO   MAROC

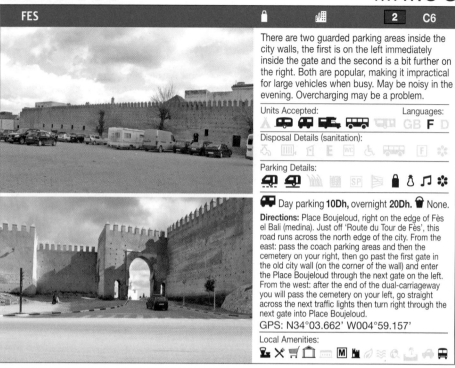

There are two guarded parking areas inside the city walls, the first is on the left immediately inside the gate and the second is a bit further on the right. Both are popular, making it impractical for large vehicles when busy. May be noisy in the evening. Overcharging may be a problem.

Units Accepted: Languages:
GB **F** D

Disposal Details (sanitation):

Parking Details:

Day parking **10Dh,** overnight **20Dh.** None.

Directions: Place Boujeloud, right on the edge of Fès el Bali (medina). Just off 'Route du Tour de Fès', this road runs across the north edge of the city. From the east: pass the coach parking areas and then the cemetery on your right, then go past the first gate in the old city wall (on the corner of the wall) and enter the Place Boujeloud through the next gate on the left. From the west: after the end of the dual-carriageway you will pass the cemetery on your left, go straight across the next traffic lights then turn right through the next gate into Place Boujeloud.

GPS: N34°03.662' W004°59.157'

Local Amenities:

The guardians were friendly and helpful. The parking area is located close to the city walls and the old medina of Fès el Bali. There is plenty of room for large motorhomes.

Units Accepted: Languages:
GB **F** D

Disposal Details (sanitation):

Parking Details:

Day parking **10Dh,** overnight **20Dh.** None.

Directions: Route du Tour de Fès. Right on the edge of Fès el Bali (medina) beside the road which runs across the north of the city, From the east: pass the coach parking areas and then the cemetery on your right, then carry on along the city walls until they turn away to the left. Parking area is a short distance on the left, opposite another part of the cemetery. From the west: after the end of the dual carriageway you will see the round tower at the corner of the city walls on the right and then the cemetery on your left, the parking is opposite the cemetery. The guardian will probably flag you down.

GPS: N34°03.662' W004°59.157'

Local Amenities:

MOULAY IDRISS (VOLUBILIS) 7 C6

Overnight stays are not permitted at the parking for Volubilis, as an alternative, Mohamed Samir offers a place alongside his stall or opposite, amongst the olive trees. Mohamed speaks French; his brother is a teacher who speaks some English.

Units Accepted: Languages: GB F

Disposal Details (sanitation):

Parking Details: SP

3. A gift of 10 – 20Dh would be acceptable. None.

Directions: Take the Volubilis turn off the N13 and just after the turning stop and see Mohamed Samir the souvenir seller.

GPS: N34°04.373' W005°32.677'

Local Amenities:

Tourist attractions 1km.

TANGER (KSAR-ES-SEGHIR) 13 A6

This parking area is next to a small fishing port and overlooks the sandy bay. A Gendarmerie post at the port entrance provides a sense of security. It's a short walk into the town where there are a few shops, several restaurants and cafés and a ruined Portuguese fort. Overnight parking has been tolerated here in the past and readers must make their own assessment.

Units Accepted: Languages: GB F D

Disposal Details (sanitation):

Parking Details:

5. Free. None.

Directions: Ksar-es-Seghir. Located halfway between Ceuta and Tanger on the coast road. In the town take the road signed 'Café Restaurant Port Ksar Seghir'. The parking area is on the right just before the port entrance.

GPS: N35°50.945' W005°33.649'

Local Amenities:

All approx 500m in town.

CAP SPARTEL   15   A6

At the viewpoint next to the Cap Spartel lighthouse small parking area. There are cafés and souvenir sellers nearby.

Units Accepted: Languages:

Disposal Details (sanitation):

Parking Details:

5. Free. None.

Directions: Cap Spartel lighthouse parking. Follow directions to Camping Achakkar, continue on to the end of the road at Cap Spartel, limited parking spaces opposite the café, next to the lighthouse.

GPS: N35°47.589' W005°55.446'

Local Amenities:

CAP SPARTEL   16   A6

Grassy parking areas overlooking the beach.

Units Accepted: Languages:

Disposal Details (sanitation):

Parking Details:

Negotiate with guardians (around 10Dh/day). None.

Directions: Achakkar day parking. Follow directions to Camping Achakkar, after the campsite turn right at the roundabout and the parking places are on the left in about 1.5km.

GPS: N35°45.916' W005°56.097'

Local Amenities:

CAP SPARTEL ☼ 🔔↘ **17** A6

Plenty of parking alongside the track to the beach and restaurant. A military post just beyond the restaurant provides a sense of security. Overnight parking has been tolerated in the past and readers must make their own assessment.

Units Accepted: Languages:
△ 🚐 🚙 🚍 🚌 ⌷⌷ **GB** **F** **D**

Disposal Details (sanitation):
♿ ▥ 🏠 E WC ♿ 🚰 F ⚶

Parking Details:
🚐 🚐 🔥 🏢 SP 🏴 🎒 🎵 ❀

🚐 10. Free. 🔔 None.

Directions: Plage Achakkar. Follow directions to Camping Achakkar, the beach is about 2.5km further on, go past the beach and take the track on the left towards the restaurant. Parking is along the wide track.

GPS: N35°40.915' W005°55.777'

Local Amenities:
🍖 ✕ 🛒 🏠 ▦ **M** 🏭 ⌀ ≈ ⌀ ⬆ 🚐 🚌

SIDI KACEM 🔋 ≈ ↘ 🚐 **19** A6

Parking area controlled by the military, ask at the military post for permission to stay overnight. There is a view over the beach and space for a handful of motorhomes but there are no facilities. Overnight parking is not permitted at any of the other beachside parking areas.

Units Accepted: Languages:
△ 🚐 🚙 🚍 🚌 ⌷⌷ GB **F** D

Disposal Details (sanitation):
♿ ▥ 🏠 E WC ♿ 🚰 F ⚶

Parking Details:
🚐 🚐 🔥 🏢 SP 🏴 🎒 🎵 ❀

🚐 6. Free. 🔔 None.

Directions: Plage Sidi Kacem. Follow directions to Camping Achakkar, just before the campsite take the road to the left, signed 'Sidi Kacem'. After a few km, where the road turns away from the coast, carry straight on up the rough track to the gravel parking area.

GPS: N35°43.151' W005°56.861'

Local Amenities:
🍖 ✕ 🛒 🏠 ▦ M 🏭 ⌀ ≈ ⌀ ⬆ 🚐 🚌

ASILAH   20   B6

Large open grass parking area right on the beach. The guardian assured us that overnight parking was possible for an unspecified fee. Beach toilets were locked at the time of our visit but guardian would open them on request.

Units Accepted: Languages: GB **F** D

Disposal Details (sanitation):

Parking Details:

100. Pay. Water and toilets on request. Toilet disposal in toilet on request.

Directions: Briech Plage. About 5km north of Asilah turn off the N1 coast road opposite the Hotel Village Touristique de Briech.

GPS: N35°32.069' W006°00.371'

Local Amenities:

All 5km in Asilah.

ASILAH   22   B6

Located alongside the old medina this flat parking area has views over the adjacent fishing port and a small sandy bay. The Medina has been extensively renovated and, although mainly residential, is a pleasant place to go exploring. The guardian will lift a manhole cover for cassette, grey and black waste emptying. This is a popular overnight stop and may be full at times. Authorities allow overnight parking here since the closure of the two town campsites.

Units Accepted: Languages: **GB F** D

Disposal Details (sanitation):

Parking Details:

50. 20 Dh. Ask guardian.

Directions: Parking du Port. Coming from the north as enter town cross the river bear right at the traffic lights. From the south, go straight through the town and then turn sharp left just before the river bridge. Parking is in front of the old medina walls in about 500m.

GPS: N35°28.202' W006°02.312'

Local Amenities:

All 300m in town.

LARACHE

23 B6

Parking directly on the beach, on hard sand or concrete apron. Beach toilets open in summer but there is water and toilets available at café opposite the beach road (ask guardian). Nominally free in winter but the guardian expects a 'gift'. The Roman ruins of Lixus are just at the turning off the main road. Flamingos are often seen on the adjacent saltpans.

Units Accepted: Languages:

F

Disposal Details (sanitation):

Parking Details:

25, Free. Ask for water and toilets.

Directions: Lixus. Take the N1 north from Larache, just after the salt pans on the left take the left turn signed for 'Ras El Rmel' and 'Lixus', parking on the beach in about 5km.

GPS: N35°12.271' W006°08.939'

Local Amenities:

Provisions, restaurant 200m. Supermarket, bank, public transport Larache.

SALE

30 C5

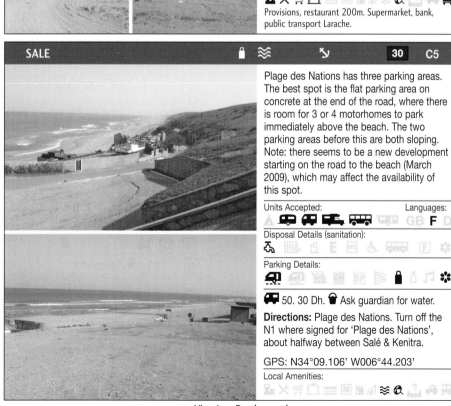

Plage des Nations has three parking areas. The best spot is the flat parking area on concrete at the end of the road, where there is room for 3 or 4 motorhomes to park immediately above the beach. The two parking areas before this are both sloping. Note: there seems to be a new development starting on the road to the beach (March 2009), which may affect the availability of this spot.

Units Accepted: Languages:

F

Disposal Details (sanitation):

Parking Details:

50. 30 Dh. Ask guardian for water.

Directions: Plage des Nations. Turn off the N1 where signed for 'Plage des Nations', about halfway between Salé & Kenitra.

GPS: N34°09.106' W006°44.203'

Local Amenities:

TEMARA PLAGE   31   C5

Free parking opposite the hotel St Germain De Laye. Beach showers and toilets are only available during the summer. Just behind the parking area is Camping Palmerai, which appeared to be abandoned. There appeared to be no campsite facilities or guardian.

Units Accepted: Languages:

Disposal Details (sanitation):

Parking Details:

🚐 10. Free. 🔔 None.

Directions: Temara Plage. On the R322, coming from Rabat into Temara Plage pass green sentry boxes on the right, then take 2nd right towards Hotel St Germain De Laye. Parking in front of hotel.

GPS: N33°55.835' W006°57.274'

Local Amenities:

All a few hundred metres in the town.

MOHAMMEDIA   35   C5

This is a small untidy parking place suitable for 2 or 3 motorhomes. Located in the middle of a residential area, locals gave assurance that overnight parking was ok and that security guards patrolled the area at night. There is a small shop nearby. Access to the beach is down a path between buildings.

Units Accepted: Languages:

Disposal Details (sanitation):

Parking Details:

🚐 3. Free. 🔔 None.

Directions: Coming from Rabat into Mohammedia, cross the river, and then in about 500m turn right. Parking space is in about 500m.

GPS: N33°43.224' W007°20.887'

Local Amenities:

All 1km in Mohammedia. Beaches 100m.

DAR BOUAZZA 🔒 ≋ 🍴🏘🏛 | 36 | C5

The beachfront road has guarded parking spaces and some off road parking directly on the beach. Jack Beach is a popular surf spot and the town of Dar Bouazza is very quiet in the winter but a few restaurants and a couple of surf shops were open when we visited in March.

Units Accepted: | Languages:
🚐 🚗 🚚 🚌 | GB **F** D

Disposal Details (sanitation):

Parking Details:

🚐 10. 5Dh/day +5Dh/night. 🛎 None.

Directions: Jack Beach. Follow directions to Camping International L'Oasis but carry on towards Azemmour for about 1km, turning right opposite the Shell fuel station, at the sign to 'Camping Tamaris II'. Carry straight on, turning right along the beach road.
GPS: N33°31.859' W007°49.997'

Local Amenities:

All 1km in Dar Bouazza. Beaches adjacent.

AZEMMOUR ≋ | 🍴🏛 | 39 | C4

Large parking bays just behind the beach, the area seems to be mainly occupied by holiday homes and is very quiet in winter. Overnight parking has been tolerated in the past and readers must make their own assessment.

Units Accepted: | Languages:
🚐 🚗 🚚 🚌 | GB F D

Disposal Details (sanitation):

Parking Details:

🚐 10. Free. 🛎 None.

Directions: Plage d'Azemmour. In Azemmour follow the road alongside the medina wall signed for 'Plage D'Haouza', turn right at next junction, straight over 1st roundabout, turn right at 2nd roundabout. large parking bays in 100m.
GPS: N33°18.539' W008°21.382'

Local Amenities:

All 1km in Azemmour.

EL JADIDA   ☼ ≋   ⅋ 🏢   **41**   C4

Located on a busy road in the town this on street parking provides direct access to the beach.

Units Accepted: **Languages:**

🚲 🚐 🚘 🚍 🚌   GB F D

Disposal Details (sanitation):

⚗ 🏛 🚪 E WC ♿ 🚿 F ❄

Parking Details:

🚐 🚐 📶 🏨 SP ⛳ 🛄 🍼 🎵 ✿

🚐 15. Free. 🚻 None.

Directions: Plage d'El Jadida. Heading into El Jadida from Casablanca keep right on entering town to follow the beachside road 'Boulevard de la Plage'. Parking each side of the road near the Hotel Ibis.

GPS: N33°14.903' W008°29.450'

Local Amenities:

🐟 ✕ 🛒 🏚 ▭ Ⓜ 🏍 ◇ ≋ ⌖ ⚓ 🚲 🚌

All 1km in El Jadida. Beaches adjacent.

SIDI BOUZID   ☼ ≋   ⅋ 🏛   **42**   C4

This area is mainly occupied with summer holiday homes and is quiet in winter. There is on street parking with direct access to the beach.

Units Accepted: **Languages:**

🚲 🚐 🚘 🚍 🚌   GB F D

Disposal Details (sanitation):

⚗ 🏛 🚪 E WC ♿ 🚿 F ❄

Parking Details:

🚐 🚐 📶 🏨 SP ⛳ 🛄 🍼 🎵 ✿

🚐 20. Free. 🚻 None.

Directions: Plage de Sidi Bouzid. On the R301 coast road just to the south of El Jadida turn right at the sign to 'Sidi Bouzid' and carry on straight through the village eventually turning left along the sea front road (one way). There are short marked bays on the right and longer bays opposite.

GPS: N33°13.568' W008°33.362'

Local Amenities:

🐟 ✕ 🛒 🏚 ▭ Ⓜ 🏍 ◇ ≋ ⌖ ⚓ 🚲 🚌

All around 1km in El Jadida. Beaches adjacent.

SIDI ABED 43 C4

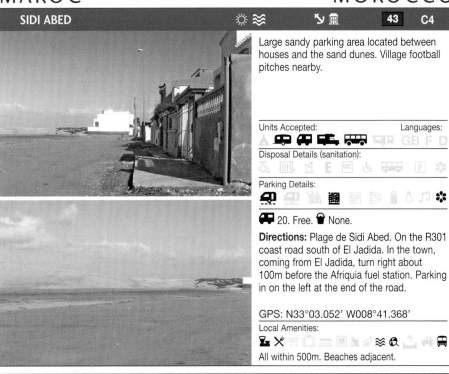

Large sandy parking area located between houses and the sand dunes. Village football pitches nearby.

Units Accepted: Languages: GB F D

Disposal Details (sanitation):

Parking Details:

20. Free. None.

Directions: Plage de Sidi Abed. On the R301 coast road south of El Jadida. In the town, coming from El Jadida, turn right about 100m before the Afriquia fuel station. Parking in on the left at the end of the road.

GPS: N33°03.052' W008°41.368'

Local Amenities:

All within 500m. Beaches adjacent.

OUALIDIA 45 D4

There are several on street and off-street guarded parking places available in the village. Park outside the campsite and inspect available places. The most popular places are around the road opposite the campsite, as there is a fine view over the lagoon. To maintain goodwill, do not park in the places that have 'no camping' signs.

Units Accepted: Languages: GB F D

Disposal Details (sanitation):

Parking Details:

30. 15Dh. Beach toilets open, but filthy and unusable, no water.

Directions: The easiest access is from the road that branches off the R301 and runs towards the coast from the southernmost edge of the town. Follow this road and turn left at the bottom and stop outside the campsite on the left in a few hundred metres.

GPS: N32°44.140' W009°02.556'

Local Amenities:

Market (souk) Sunday. All in village within 500m.

CAP BEDDOUZA ☼ ↘ 🚐 **46** D4

Roadside parking next to the beach. Moroccans use much of the area as a summer campsite, but it is very quiet in winter. Overnight parking has been tolerated in the past and readers must make their own assessment.

Units Accepted: Languages:

Disposal Details (sanitation):

Parking Details:

🚐 20. Free. 🚿 Beach toilets and showers locked in winter.
Directions: Beddouza Beach. Off the coast road south of the village. Coming from El Jadida go through the village and take the right turn after the lighthouse, signed 'Plage Beddouza'.
GPS: N32°32.930' W009°16.749'

Local Amenities:

Shop and restaurant 2km in Beddouza. Beach adjacent.

SAFI 🔒 ≋ ↘ **48** D4

Partly level parking, high up with a view to the port, town and a popular surfing spot. The guardian told us that overnight parking was no problem, and free, but readers must make their own assessment. It is busy here on fine evenings with locals and surfers.

Units Accepted: Languages:

Disposal Details (sanitation):

Parking Details:

🚐 10. Free. 🚿 None.
Directions: Plage de Safi. Coming into Safi from El Jadida on the R301 coast road, at the edge of town turn down the road alongside the Hotel Atlantique, keep left and follow the twisting road down to the parking.
GPS: N32°19.425' W009°15.569'

Local Amenities:

All 2km in Safi. Day parking and beaches adjacent. Public transport at top of road.

SOUIRIA 🔒 ⚓🏢 **50** D4

Located in this seaside village just off the seafront road, the flat parking area has space for 30 motorhomes. The only facility is drinking water from one tap. New apartments are under construction but village is very quiet in winter.

Units Accepted: Languages:

🏕️ 🚐 🚗 🚌 🚛   GB **F** D

Disposal Details (sanitation):

♿ ▥ 🔲 E 🚻 ♿ 🚽 F ❄️

Parking Details:

🚐 🚐 🕳️ 🏛️ SP 🚩 🔒 △ 🎵 ❀

🚐 30. 20Dh. 🎪 None.

Directions: Souiria. Coming from Safi on the R301 just before the village turn right, signed 'Plage' and 'Port', turn left in front of the Port and continue along the seafront, parking is in around 500m on left.

GPS: N32°02.977' W009°20.401'

Local Amenities:

🍴 ✕ 🍽️ 🏧 🏛️ M 🔭 ☀️ 🌊 🔍 🚂 🚐 🚃

MOULAY BOUZERKTOUN ☀️ ⚓📏 **51** D3

Rough beachside parking on stones, sand and grass, beside a Gendarmerie post. A pleasant quiet spot in winter with direct access to good beach that is popular with windsurfers in summer. Cafés and small shop nearby. Children are friendly and take orders for fresh bread, which they deliver the next morning. Overnight parking has been tolerated in the past and readers must make their own assessment.

Units Accepted: Languages:

△ 🏕️ 🚐 🚗 🚌 🚛   GB F D

Disposal Details (sanitation):

♿ ▥ 🔲 E 🚻 ♿ 🚽 F ❄️

Parking Details:

🚐 🚐 🕳️ 🏛️ SP 🚩 🔒 △ 🎵 ❀

🚐 20. Free. 🎪 None.

Directions: Off the R301 coast road north of Essaouira, 19km from the junction with the R207 Essaouira-Marrakech road, signed Moulay Bouzerktoun. Follow the road into the village then turn left along the rough track to the beachside parking area.

GPS: N31°38.687' W009°40.611'

Local Amenities:

🍴 ✕ 🍽️ 🏧 🏛️ M 🔭 🌊 🔍 🚂 🚐 🚃

ESSAOUIRA 🔒 ⚓ **53** D3

Tarmac parking areas with excellent beach views. Located 1km from the souks and port. Parking area floods when it rains. Beach toilets provide some services, negotiate with guardian. The sanddune parking is furthest from town and does not have a sea view but the dune prevents the virtually constant onshore wind. To maintain goodwill, do not park in the places that have 'no camping' signs and if you wish to stay the night use the campsite.

Units Accepted: Languages:

🏕️ 🚐 🚐 🚍 🚐 🚌 🚐 GB **F** D

Disposal Details (sanitation):

🚰 🏚️ 🔲 E WC ♿ 🚽 F ❄️

Parking Details:

🚐 🚐 🔥 🏨 SP 🏴 🔒 🔥 🎵 ❁

🚐 30. 20-40Dh. ☕ Continental, 1Dh.

Directions: Parking areas adjacent to beach. Most popular area is on left before the harbour car park. Also popular is parking opposite Hotel Atlas Essaouira & Spa, this area is signed no parking at night. Thirdly on road to Adagir before the small lighthouse, the large parking area is at the base of a large sanddune, was available at new year but was closed off in February. We do not recommend the harbour car park, as this gets very busy.

GPS: N31°30.144'W009°45.800'

Local Amenities:

🛒 ✕ 🍴 🏛️ 🏠 🚇 M 🕎 ⊘ ≋ ⊕ 🛠️ 🚗 🚐

SIDI KAOUKI ☀️ ⚓ 🛏️ **57** E3

Free parking place by Gendarmerie and cafés. Water is available at the nearby water tower. Beach toilets available but were closed when visited in January. Overnight parking here may be stopped because of the new campsite opening, check with Gendarmerie. Fresh bread delivered by donkey each morning, direct to your motorhome.

Units Accepted: Languages:

🏕️ 🚐 🚐 🚐 🚐 🚐 🚐 GB F D

Disposal Details (sanitation):

🚰 🏚️ 🔲 E WC ♿ 🚽 F ❄️

Parking Details:

🚐 🚐 🔥 🏨 SP 🏴 🔒 🔥 🎵 ❁

🚐 10. Free. ☕ Nearby, free.

Directions: Beach parking by Gendarmerie. Turn off the N1 Essaouira-Agadir road around 13km south of Essaouira, signed Sidi Kaouki, beach parking is alongside Gendarmerie and a collection of small cafés.

GPS: N31°21.506' W009°47.891'

Local Amenities:

🛒 ✕ 🍴 🏛️ 🏠 🚇 M 🕎 ⊘ ≋ ⊕ 🛠️ 🚗 🚐

All adjacent.

IMSOUANE ☼ ≋   ↘ ⊒   **61**   E3

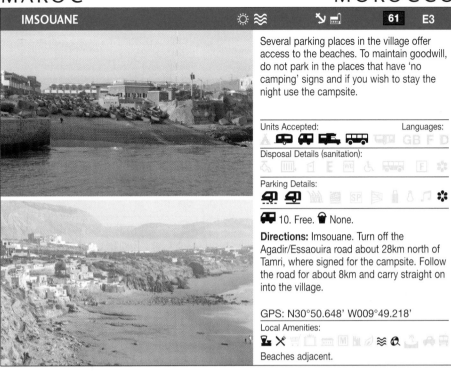

Several parking places in the village offer access to the beaches. To maintain goodwill, do not park in the places that have 'no camping' signs and if you wish to stay the night use the campsite.

Units Accepted: Languages:

🚐 🚘 🚍 🚌   GB F D

Disposal Details (sanitation):

Parking Details:

🚐 🚐   🔟. Free. ♟ None.

Directions: Imsouane. Turn off the Agadir/Essaouira road about 28km north of Tamri, where signed for the campsite. Follow the road for about 8km and carry straight on into the village.

GPS: N30°50.648' W009°49.218'

Local Amenities:

Beaches adjacent.

TAMRI ☼ ≋   ↘ ⌂   **62**   E3

This large flat parking area is high above the lagoon at the mouth of the river. It is a long walk down to the beach.

Units Accepted: Languages:

🚐 🚘 🚍 🚌   GB F D

Disposal Details (sanitation):

Parking Details:

🚐 🚐   25. Free. ♟ None.

Directions: Plage de Tamri. Travelling out of Tamri towards Essaouira the parking place is down the track on the left just after the bend at the top of the hill, opposite the buff coloured concrete wall of the water treatment works.

GPS: N30°42.683' W009°50.874'

Local Amenities:

All 2km in Tamri.

MOROCCO   MAROC

Various unguarded day parking places next to the sea, and some good surfing spots. The available places change from time to time as the entrances are sometime blocked off to discourage overnight parking. Off-site overnight parking is not recommended anywhere between here and Agadir.

Units Accepted: Languages:

🚶 🚐 🚙 🚚 🚌 🚐   GB F D

Disposal Details (sanitation):

⬦ ▥ 🚽 E WC ♿ 🚐 F ❄

Parking Details:

🚐 🚐 〰 🏛 SP ⚑ 🛢 🔥 🎵 ❀

🚐 Varies. Free. ♿ None.

Directions: Along the coast road between Cap Rhir (GPS point) and Aghroud (N30°35.943' W009°46.495') are numerous turnings off towards the sea leading to day parking locations.

GPS: N30°37.921' W009°52.908'

Local Amenities:

🛒 ✕ 🛒 🏛 ▦ M ⭙ ⌀ ≋ ⊙ ⬆ 🚗 🚐

Beachside parking by a restaurant and surf spot.

Units Accepted: Languages:

🚶 🚐 🚙 🚚 🚌 🚐   GB **F** D

Disposal Details (sanitation):

⬦ ▥ 🚽 E WC ♿ 🚐 F ❄

Parking Details:

🚐 🚐 〰 🏛 SP ⚑ 🛢 🔥 🎵 ❀

🚐 25. 5Dh. ♿ None.

Directions: Route de Taghazout. Plage Abouda. About 4km north of Taghazout turn off where signed, next to large beachside restaurant.

GPS: N30°34.253' W009°44.677'

Local Amenities:

🛒 ✕ 🛒 🏛 ▦ M ⭙ ⌀ ≋ ⊙ ⬆ 🚗 🚐

Restaurant adjacent.

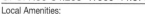

AGHROUD ☼ ⟍ ⌂ **65** E5

Large beachside parking, more parking places are located just to the north of the village.

Units Accepted: Languages:

Disposal Details (sanitation):

Parking Details:

🚐 25. Free. ☂ None.

Directions: Route de Taghazout. Plage Aghroud 2. About 1km south of Aghroud, signed.

GPS: N30°35.935' W009°46.498'

Local Amenities:

1km in village.

TAGHAZOUT ☼ ≋ ⟍ 🛒 **67** E3

Taghazout is a popular surfing centre and busy even in winter. There are several parking places in the village. The Panorama surf spot is just off the road to the south (signed), there is parking outside the surf shop.

Units Accepted: Languages:

Disposal Details (sanitation):

Parking Details:

🚐 25. Free. ☂ None.

Directions: Taghazout is on the N1 about 18km north of Agadir.

GPS: N30°32.638' W009°42.452'

Local Amenities:

All adjacent.

TAGHAZOUT   ☼ ≋   ⚓ ⌂   **68**   E3

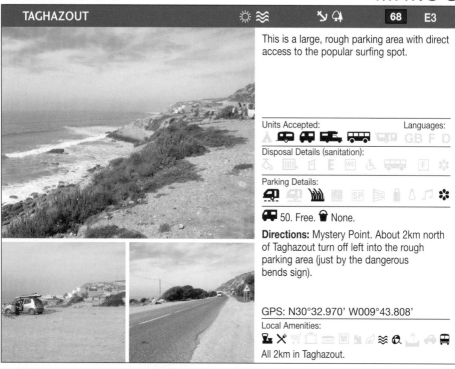

This is a large, rough parking area with direct access to the popular surfing spot.

Units Accepted: Languages:

🅰 🚐 🚗 🚙 🚌 🚐   GB F D

Disposal Details (sanitation):

⚐ 🏢 ⚑ E 🚾 ♿ �   F ❋

Parking Details:

🚐 🚐 ⑉ ▥ SP ⚑ 🛢 ⚱ ♪ ✿

🚐 50. Free. ♟ None.

Directions: Mystery Point. About 2km north of Taghazout turn off left into the rough parking area (just by the dangerous bends sign).

GPS: N30°32.970' W009°43.808'

Local Amenities:

🛒 ✕ 🛒 🏠 🚉 Ⓜ 🛍 ⊘ ≋ ⊙ ⬆ 🚚 🚌

All 2km in Taghazout.

TAGHAZOUT   ☼   ⚓ ⌂   **69**   E3

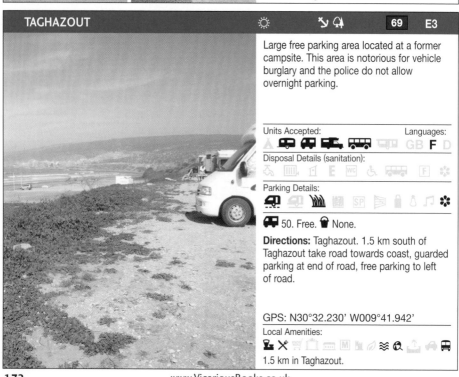

Large free parking area located at a former campsite. This area is notorious for vehicle burglary and the police do not allow overnight parking.

Units Accepted: Languages:

🅰 🚐 🚗 🚙 🚌 🚐   GB **F** D

Disposal Details (sanitation):

⚐ 🏢 ⚑ E 🚾 ♿ �   F ❋

Parking Details:

🚐 🚐 ⑉ ▥ SP ⚑ 🛢 ⚱ ♪ ✿

🚐 50. Free. ♟ None.

Directions: Taghazout. 1.5 km south of Taghazout take road towards coast, guarded parking at end of road, free parking to left of road.

GPS: N30°32.230' W009°41.942'

Local Amenities:

🛒 ✕ 🛒 🏠 🚉 Ⓜ 🛍 ⊘ ≋ ⊙ ⬆ 🚚 🚌

1.5 km in Taghazout.

MIRLEFT   78   F3

This flat parking area is located just outside the small fishing port. Overnight parking has been tolerated in the past and readers must make their own assessment.

Units Accepted: **Languages:**

Disposal Details (sanitation):

Parking Details:

🚐 10. Free. 🛈 None.

Directions: Point de Debarquement Sidi Boulfdail. About 11km north of Mirleft, just south of the village of Sidi Boulfdail, take the turn towards the coast, signed 'Point de Débarquement Aménagé de Sidi Boulfdail'. Parking is on the left in front of the port entrance.

GPS: N29°40.054' W009°58.900'

Local Amenities:

MIRLEFT   80   F3

Located in a small bay this is day parking right on the beach.

Units Accepted: **Languages:**

Disposal Details (sanitation):

Parking Details:

🚐 25. Free. 🛈 None.

Directions: Plage des Marabouts, Sidi Mohamed ou Abdallah. About 6km south of Mirleft, the parking is between the road and the beach.

GPS: N29°34.161' W010°03.072'

Local Amenities:

MIRLEFT   🔒 ≋   ⚓   **81**   F3

Parking on the concrete apron amongst the boats right in this tiny fishing port, just above the rocks. Only a few motorhomes are allowed, check with the port office before staying overnight.

Units Accepted: **Languages:**

🚗 🚐 🚑 🚙 🚌 🚎   GB **F** D

Disposal Details (sanitation):

Parking Details:

🚐 5. Free. 🔔 None.

Directions: Point de Debarquement Aftess Rkount. About 20km north of Sidi Ifni, just north of the village of Aftess Rkount, take the turn towards the coast, signed 'Point de Debarquement Aménagé de Rkount'. Follow the road down to the small fishing port. Parking is on the concrete area facing the sea on the far side of the slipway. Boats may obstruct access, there is limited manoeuvring space and large motorhomes will have difficulty crossing the slipway.

GPS: N29°30.318' W010°04.557'

Local Amenities:

LA PLAGE BLANCHE   ☼   ⚓🏕   **86**   F2

This exposed parking area is located right above the huge Plage Blanche. The site suffers from wind blown sand but there is a steep track down towards the Oued to a more sheltered spot. Children take orders for fresh bread and bring it to your motorhome in the morning. Overnight parking has been tolerated in the past and readers must make their own assessment.

Units Accepted: **Languages:**

🏕 🚗 🚐 🚑 🚌 🚎   GB **F** D

Disposal Details (sanitation):

Parking Details:

🚐 100. Free. 🔔 None.

Directions: La Plage Blanche. In Guelmim take the road towards Sidi Ifni, just at the edge of Guelmim take the left turn signed 'Plage Blanche'. Follow the Plage Blanche signs to the coast. The parking area is at the end of the tarmac road.

GPS: N28°57.818' W010°36.120'

Local Amenities:

OUED CHBIKA
☼ ⚓ **90** G2

This is a superb location, overlooking the lagoon. Unrestricted parking on hard sand and there is a fresh water spring nearby. Gendarmerie post at the top of the hill. Overnight parking has been tolerated in the past and readers must make their own assessment.

Units Accepted: Languages: GB F D

Disposal Details (sanitation):

Parking Details:

🚐 20. Free. ♿ None.

Directions: Oued Chbika. Road from Tan Tan to Tarfaya. Around 31km from Tan Tan Plage towards Tarfaya.

GPS: N28°17.466' W011°32.198'

Local Amenities:

OUED MA FATMA
🔋 ⚓ **91** G2

Overnight parking on cliffs overlooking mouth of Oued. We didn't visit this site because the track was impassable due to heavy rain at the time, but we understand that it costs 5Dh per night and there is water and toilets available. Overnight parking has been tolerated in the past and readers must make their own assessment.

Units Accepted: Languages: GB **F** D

Disposal Details (sanitation):

Parking Details:

🚐 Unknown. 5Dh. ♿ Water 20Dh.

Directions: Oued Ma Fatma. Road from Tan Tan to Tarfaya. Roughly 60km south of Tan Tan Plage the parking is signed 'Parking Payant' on the right just after crossing the Oued.

GPS: N28°12.300' W011°46.970'

Local Amenities:

Library picture..

AKHFENNIR 🔒 ⚡ 🚿 **92** G1

A remote, exposed spot with a superb view overlooking the lagoon. The ground is rocky and uneven. Overnight parking is permitted at the Parc National Khenifiss but a free permit must be obtained in advance from the National Park office in Akhfennir. Locals offer boat hire and fishing trips on the lagoon.

Units Accepted: Languages: GB **F** D

Disposal Details (sanitation):

Parking Details:

🚐 30. Free. ⚲ None.

Directions: Lagune de Khenifiss. Turn off the N1 where signed, about 20km past Akhfennir towards Tarfaya

GPS: N28°01.709' W012°14.396'

Local Amenities:

TARFAYA 🔒 ⚡ 🚿 **93** G1

Relatively flat parking area right next to the sea, cliffs and a good beach for fishing. There are no services, and it is an exposed location. Overnight parking has been tolerated in the past and readers must make their own assessment.

Units Accepted: Languages: GB **F** D

Disposal Details (sanitation):

Parking Details:

🚐 10. 20Dh. ⚲ None.

Directions: Tarfaya. On the N1 coming from Tan Tan Plage, turn left down the track where signed, about 6km before the turning for Tarfaya.

GPS: N27°57.527' W012°51.709'

Local Amenities:

FOUM EL OUED   96   G1

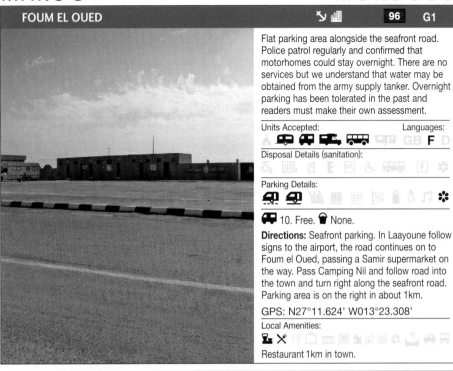

Flat parking area alongside the seafront road. Police patrol regularly and confirmed that motorhomes could stay overnight. There are no services but we understand that water may be obtained from the army supply tanker. Overnight parking has been tolerated in the past and readers must make their own assessment.

Units Accepted: Languages: GB **F** D

Disposal Details (sanitation):

Parking Details:

10. Free. None.

Directions: Seafront parking. In Laayoune follow signs to the airport, the road continues on to Foum el Oued, passing a Samir supermarket on the way. Pass Camping Nil and follow road into the town and turn right along the seafront road. Parking area is on the right in about 1km.

GPS: N27°11.624' W013°23.308'

Local Amenities:

Restaurant 1km in town.

TAFRAOUT   104   F4

Huge 'guarded' parking area to the left of the track, which crosses the open ground. The area to the right, between the track and the campsite is controlled by Camping les Trois Palmiers. A guardian collects 10Dh per night; the actual security provided is questionable.

Units Accepted: Languages: GB **F** D

Disposal Details (sanitation):

Parking Details:

100s. 10Dh. None.

Directions: On the R104 coming from Tiznit bear left on entering the town, site is on the left about 500m before Camping les Trois Palmiers.

GPS: N29°43.272' W008°58.872'

Local Amenities:

All 500m in town.

TAROUDANT   🔒   🏢   **106**   E4

Motorhome parking is permitted in two places: The first (at the GPS position) near the Hotel Palais Salam, the second, larger area is just around the corner near the Bab Lahjer. Cassette emptying and water container filling is possible at both parking areas, ask the guardians. Both parking areas are convenient for a walk to Taroudant medina, which is fairly compact and manageable.

Units Accepted: Languages:

   GB **F** D

Disposal Details (sanitation):

Parking Details:

🚐 50. 20Dh/24 hours. 🛈 Poss.

Directions: Parking on left, just after the Hotel Palais Salam, by the city walls. West: Follow the old city walls on your left in the town until they turn away to the left, and then at the roundabout bear left to follow the walls on your left again. Parking on left after Hotel Palais Salam. East: Look for the old city walls on your right, as soon as you see them (at the second roundabout), turn sharp right. Parking on left after the Hotel Palais Salam. For the second, larger, parking place continue past the first, round the left hand bend, the parking is on the right at the end of the road.

GPS: N30°28.582' W008°52.242'

Local Amenities:

All a few hundred metres, in the town.

MARRAKECH   🔒   🏢   **108**   D4

A flat P shaped walled parking area far enough away from the main road to be quiet and the main square is just 5 mins walk. This guarded parking area was allowing motorhomes to stop overnight. Readers must make their own assessment. Warning! Chained dogs guard some of the cars at the rear of the car park.

Units Accepted: Languages:

      GB **F** D

Disposal Details (sanitation):

Parking Details:

🚐 10. 50Dh. 🛈 None.

Directions: Parking de la Koutoubia, Ave Mohammed V (203). Enter Marrakech from the South on the 203, follow this road past the Koutoubia Minaret and mosque on your left. At the large roundabout turn right round and travel back the way you have come, past the cyber park towards the Koutoubia Minaret. When you can see the top of the minaret, behind trees, turn right sign posted 'P' into one-way street. 100m from turn, at the rear of Koutoubia mosque, the parking is on the right. Motorhome parking is at the rear of the car park. Max 9m.

GPS: N31°37.462' W007°59.677'

Local Amenities:

All 300m.

AIT BENHADDOU   114   E5

This is the main parking area for visiting the Aït Benhaddou Kasbah. Overnight parking by arrangement with the guardian. Access to the Kasbah is down the track in the far left corner of the parking area. Cafés, souvenirs, internet kiosk, all nearby.

Units Accepted: Languages:

GB **F** D

Disposal Details (sanitation):

Parking Details:

🚐 10. Around 20Dh. 🚻 None.

Directions: Parking in front of Hotel la Kasbah. On the right just as you enter the village of Aït Benhaddou, signed 'L'Entree Principal Du Site Aït Benhaddou'.

GPS: N31°02.558' W007°07.753'

Local Amenities:

All within 500m.

OUARZAZATE   117   E5

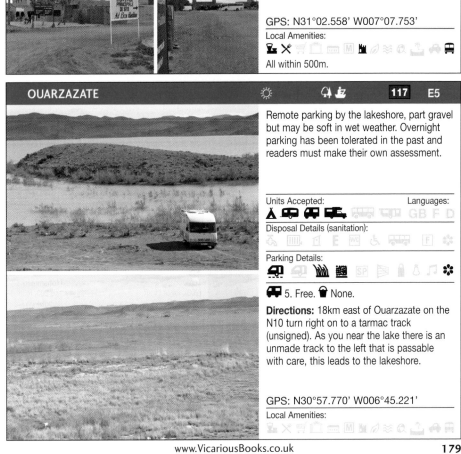

Remote parking by the lakeshore, part gravel but may be soft in wet weather. Overnight parking has been tolerated in the past and readers must make their own assessment.

Units Accepted: Languages:

GB F D

Disposal Details (sanitation):

Parking Details:

🚐 5. Free. 🚻 None.

Directions: 18km east of Ouarzazate on the N10 turn right on to a tarmac track (unsigned). As you near the lake there is an unmade track to the left that is passable with care, this leads to the lakeshore.

GPS: N30°57.770' W006°45.221'

Local Amenities:

NZALA 🔒 ♠ **139** D7

This is effectively a zoo for native Saharan species, there is an Auberge attached and motorhomes are welcome to park overnight. It was closed for refurbishment when we passed in March 2009 but the guardian informed us that we would still be able to park in the compound overnight. Showers and toilets are available when the park is open.

Units Accepted: Languages:

GB F D

Disposal Details (sanitation):

Parking Details:

🚐 50. Unknown. ♛ Showers.

Directions: Parc Animalier de Nzala, Nzala. On the N13 between Midelt and Ar Rachida. About 45km south of Midelt.
Tel: 0535 589626

GPS: N32°29.068' W004°29.382'

Local Amenities:

OUAOUMANA ☼ ♠ ⚓ **143** C6

This large stony parking area is alongside the lake and an abandoned attempt to set up a campsite and café. Locals seem to use the lakeside site to wash their vehicles but otherwise it's a very peaceful location. Overnight parking has been tolerated in the past and readers must make their own assessment.

Units Accepted: Languages:

GB F D

Disposal Details (sanitation):

Parking Details:

🚐 20. Free. ♛ None.

Directions: Barrage Ahmed el Hansali. Off the N8 between Kasbah Tadla and Khenifra about 5km west of Ouaoumana. Coming from Ouaoumana the turning is on the right between two buildings immediately after a sharp left hand bend at the top of a hill. Coming from Kasbah Tadla the turning is about 7km after the turning signed to the Barrage. The rough track to the lakeside is passable with care by most motorhomes but those with low ground clearance or long rear overhang may have difficulty.

GPS: N32°42.785' W005°51.007'

Local Amenities:

All 5km in Ouaoumana.

BIN EL OUIDANE　　　　　　　144　D6

This attractive lakeside spot is on the water's edge, when the reservoir is full. Guardian charges 20Dh per night, there are no services. Gite d'Etap Chez les Berberes, about 200m away offers fishing, trekking and kayaking see www.littlemorocco.co.uk.

Units Accepted:　　　　　　　Languages:

Disposal Details (sanitation):

Parking Details:

🚐 6. 20Dh None.

Directions: Old boatyard. On the N8 about 14km west of Beni Mellal, take the R304 turning to Afourer, follow the road all the way to the dam. Cross the dam, go through the tunnel then bear left along the road that goes alongside the lake. In about 2km there is an old boatyard on the left with room for 5 or 6 motorhomes to park beside the lake.

GPS: N32°05.214' W006°27.807'

Local Amenities:

Vicarious Books

All The Aires
FRANCE

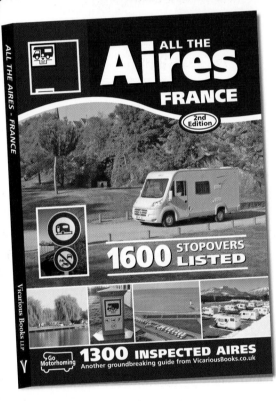

- More Aires than any other guide
- Over 1300 inspected and photographed
- Easy directions, on-site GPS co-ordinates
- Directions with road names, numbers and postcodes
- Aires for big motorhomes

only **£14.99**
inc UK P&P

NEW IMPROVED MAPPING

In France, motorhomes have the privilege of staying on 'Aires de Service pour Camping Car'. These are special areas providing facilities for motorhomes in the form of overnight parking and/or service point for water collection and disposal of waste fluids. These can be free or cost a few Euros. Aires symbolise the freedom of motorhoming. You are welcomed into local communities, where you can stay overnight at unique locations unavailable to other travellers.

To order, give us a call or visit our website to buy online.

0131 208 3333 **www.VicariousBooks.co.uk**

INDEX BY TOWN

INDEX BY TOWN

INDEX BY CAMPSITE

INDEX BY CAMPSITE

CAMPSITE SUBMISSION FORM

Please use this form to update the site information in this guide. We particularly need good photographs that represent the site. Nominations for new sites are very welcome. If site is already listed, complete only sections where changes apply. Please fill in answers in capital letters and circle appropriate symbols.

Town/Village:

Road name/number:

Units accepted: *Please circle 1 or more symbols as appropriate*

🔺 Tent   🚐 Touring caravan   🚐 Motorhome 6m

🚛 Motorhome 6m-8   🚌 Large motorhomes 8m +   🚙 Holiday accommodation for hire

Parking Type:

🔒 Guarded   ≈ Surf   ☀ Day parking   **Campsite:** _____

Ambience (type of area):

🌴 Coastal   🏢 Urban   🏠 Village   🐖 Farm

🏛 Residential   🌳 Rural   🚢 Riverside or lakeside 🏃 Park

Page Number: **Number of Spaces:**   **Cost:**

Facilities:

_____ No. of pitches   🚐 Hard standing pitches   🚐 Level pitches   🌾 Grass

_____ No. Tent pitches   SP Shaded parking   ⚑ Fenced   🔒 Guarded

▓ Sand   🕯 Illuminated   🎵 Noisy   ✳ Open all Year

Languages and credit cards and Euros accepted:

| **GB** English | **F** French | **D** German | **E** Spanish |
| **I** Italian | **S** Swedish | **CC** Credit cards | Euros |

Service Point type: **Cost:**

Disposal Details (sanitation):

🚰 Water   🚱 Non drinking water   **E** Electric hook up   ▥ Grey water disposal

MB Motorhome toilet waste disposal   MG Motorhome grey water disposal   🚽 Toilet disposal

F Free of charge   🚌 Large motorhomes

WC Toilets   ♂ Male   ♀ Female   ♿ Disabled toilet

S Standard   **C** Continental   🚿 Showers   **H** Hot   ❄ Cold   **Cost:**

Campsite amenities:

▣ Laundry   🧽 Dishwashing facilities   🛒 Shop   🏊 Swimming
                                                                      pool
✗ Restaurant   ⓘ Internet available   WiFi WiFi available

Local amenities:

🪣 Provisions   🚙 4x4 trips   🛒 Supermarket   🏦 Bank ATM

🏪 Camping shop   **M** Market (souk) 🏰 Tourist attractions 🏕 Camel trips

🌿 Gas   🚌 Public transport 🏖 Beach

Please turn over

CAMPSITE SUBMISSION FORM

Directions - Brief, specific directions to Campsite:

GPS Co-ordinates in the following format: N49°14.988' W000°16.838'

Information - Brief description of location and amenities:

☐ ☐ ☐

Photo(s) included None Emailed Picture posted with form

email pictures to: aires@vicariousbooks.co.uk

Name and email or address - so information can be credited:

Please use a separate form for each Campsite. Send completed forms to:

Vicarious Books, 62 Tontine Street, Folkestone, Kent, CT20 1JP

aires@vicariousbooks.co.uk

Thank you very much for your time.

By supplying details and photography you are giving unrestricted publication and reproduction rights to Vicarious Books Ltd.

CAMPSITE SUBMISSION FORM

Please use this form to update the site information in this guide. We particularly need good photographs that represent the site. Nominations for new sites are very welcome. If site is already listed, complete only sections where changes apply. Please fill in answers in capital letters and circle appropriate symbols.

Town/Village:

Road name/number:

Units accepted: *Please circle 1 or more symbols as appropriate*

- Tent
- Touring caravan
- Motorhome 6m
- Motorhome 6m-8
- Large motorhomes 8m +
- Holiday accommodation for hire

Parking Type:

- Guarded
- Surf
- Day parking   **Campsite:** _____

Ambience (type of area):

- Coastal
- Urban
- Village
- Farm
- Residential
- Rural
- Riverside or lakeside
- Park

Page Number: **Number of Spaces:**   **Cost:**

Facilities:

- _____ No. of pitches
- Hard standing pitches
- Level pitches
- Grass
- _____ No. Tent pitches
- SP Shaded parking
- Fenced
- Guarded
- Sand
- Illuminated
- Noisy
- Open all Year

Languages and credit cards and Euros accepted:

GB English	**F** French	**D** German	**E** Spanish
I Italian	**S** Swedish	**CC** Credit cards	Euros

Service Point type: **Cost:**

Disposal Details (sanitation):

- Water
- Non drinking water
- **E** Electric hook up
- Grey water disposal
- MB Motorhome toilet waste disposal
- MG Motorhome grey water disposal
- Toilet disposal
- **F** Free of charge
- Large motorhomes
- WC Toilets
- Male
- Female
- Disabled toilet
- **S** Standard
- **C** Continental
- Showers
- **H** Hot
- Cold   **Cost:** _____

Campsite amenities:

- Laundry
- Dishwashing facilities
- Shop
- Swimming pool
- Restaurant
- Internet available
- WiFi WiFi available

Local amenities:

- Provisions
- 4x4 trips
- Supermarket
- Bank ATM
- Camping shop
- M Market (souk)
- Tourist attractions
- Camel trips
- Gas
- Public transport
- Beach

Please turn over

CAMPSITE SUBMISSION FORM

Directions - Brief, specific directions to Campsite:

GPS Co-ordinates in the following format: N49°14.988' W000°16.838'

Information - Brief description of location and amenities:

☐   ☐   ☐

Photo(s) included   None   Emailed   Picture posted with form

email pictures to: aires@vicariousbooks.co.uk

Name and email or address - so information can be credited:

Please use a separate form for each Campsite. Send completed forms to:

Vicarious Books, 62 Tontine Street, Folkestone, Kent, CT20 1JP

aires@vicariousbooks.co.uk

Thank you very much for your time.

By supplying details and photography you are giving unrestricted publication and reproduction rights to Vicarious Books Ltd.

CAMPSITE SUBMISSION FORM

Please use this form to update the site information in this guide. We particularly need good photographs that represent the site. Nominations for new sites are very welcome. If site is already listed, complete only sections where changes apply. Please fill in answers in capital letters and circle appropriate symbols.

Town/Village:

Road name/number:

Units accepted: *Please circle 1 or more symbols as appropriate*

Tent   Touring caravan   Motorhome 6m

Motorhome 6m-8   Large motorhomes 8m +   Holiday accommodation for hire

Parking Type:

Guarded   Surf   Day parking   **Campsite:**

Ambience (type of area):

Coastal   Urban   Village   Farm

Residential   Rural   Riverside or lakeside   Park

Page Number: **Number of Spaces:**   **Cost:**

Facilities:

No. of pitches   Hard standing pitches   Level pitches   Grass

No. Tent pitches   SP Shaded parking   Fenced   Guarded

Sand   Illuminated   Noisy   Open all Year

Languages and credit cards and Euros accepted:

GB English   **F** French   **D** German   **E** Spanish

I Italian   **S** Swedish   **CC** Credit cards   Euros

Service Point type: **Cost:**

Disposal Details (sanitation):

Water   Non drinking water   **E** Electric hook up   Grey water disposal

MB Motorhome toilet waste disposal   MG Motorhome grey water disposal   Toilet disposal

F Free of charge   Large motorhomes

WC Toilets   Male   Female   Disabled toilet

S Standard   **C** Continental   Showers   **H** Hot   Cold   **Cost:**

Campsite amenities:

Laundry   Dishwashing facilities   Shop   Swimming pool

Restaurant   Internet available   WiFi WiFi available

Local amenities:

Provisions   4x4 trips   Supermarket   Bank ATM

Camping shop   M Market (souk)   Tourist attractions   Camel trips

Gas   Public transport   Beach

Please turn over

CAMPSITE SUBMISSION FORM

Directions - Brief, specific directions to Campsite:

GPS Co-ordinates in the following format: N49°14.988' W000°16.838'

Information - Brief description of location and amenities:

☐   ☐   ☐

Photo(s) included   None   Emailed   Picture posted with form

email pictures to: aires@vicariousbooks.co.uk

Name and email or address - so information can be credited:

Please use a separate form for each Campsite. Send completed forms to:

Vicarious Books, 62 Tontine Street, Folkestone, Kent, CT20 1JP

aires@vicariousbooks.co.uk

Thank you very much for your time.

By supplying details and photography you are giving unrestricted publication and reproduction rights to Vicarious Books Ltd.